Seeking a
Simpler Spirit

SEEKING A
Simpler Spirit

An 8~Week Guide toward a
Lifelong Relationship with God

DEBORAH DeFORD

The Reader's Digest Association, Inc.
Pleasantville, NY/Montreal

A **Reader's Digest Simpler Life**™ Book

Conceived and written by Deborah DeFord

Reader's Digest General Books

Editorial Director, *History, Religion,*
and Reference Books Edmund H. Harvey, Jr.

Design Director Irene Ledwith

Project Designer Barbara Lapic

Editorial Coordinator Diane Hoffman

Vice President, Editor-in-Chief Christopher Cavanaugh

Art Director Joan Mazzeo

Contributors

Illustrations Charlene Rendeiro

Copy Editor Gina E. Grant

Text Copyright © 1999 Deborah DeFord

Copyright © 1999 The Reader's Digest Association, Inc.

Library of Congress Cataloging-in-Publication Data

DeFord, Deborah H.

    Seeking a simpler spirit : an 8-week guide toward a lifelong
relationship with God / Deborah DeFord.

      p. cm.

    ISBN 0-7621-0128-8

    1. Spiritual life—Christianity.   I. Title.

    BV4501.2.D4315 1999

    291.4'4—dc21   98-50304

Printed in the United States of America

To my husband, Ron

CONTENTS

CHAPTER ONE

Beginnings

Five Essentials for Seeking God *10*

time ~ space ~ hunger ~ openness ~ commitment

CHAPTER TWO

Who Am I?

Faces of the Sincere Seeker *42*

the believer ~ the child ~ the lover

CHAPTER THREE

Are You There, God?

Road Maps and Signposts *68*

nature ~ Scripture ~ human giftedness ~ pleasures ~ pains

CHAPTER FOUR

The Practice of Seeking

Elements of Discipline *98*

orientation ~ observation ~ concentration
application ~ heart of discipline

CHAPTER FIVE

 Standing on Holy Ground

Aspects of Intimate Worship   *126*

silence ~ shouts ~ ritual actions

CHAPTER SIX

Dialogue with God

Attitudes of Prayer   *152*

joy ~ gratitude ~ patience ~ persistence ~ constancy

CHAPTER SEVEN

Learning to Fly

When the Road Is Blocked   *182*

falling rocks ~ barriers we build ~
washouts ~ breakdowns

CHAPTER EIGHT

Transformations

The Nature of Our Changes   *212*

new eyes ~ new heart ~ new hands

This is a book for seekers.

You may come to the quest with a lifelong history of religious involvement. Or you may be new to the idea of seeking to bring God into your daily life. This book asks only that you believe God to be personal and present in human lives, and One who welcomes our search for a divine connection.

This is a book for people longing to tap the deep wellsprings of their spirits. We are pelted daily by messages that promise peace, prosperity, and a happily-ever-after ending to our personal stories. Yet few, if any, of these messages provide reliable guideposts to fulfillment, peace, or joy. In the pages that follow, you will find a realistic, uncomplicated approach to discovering our souls' true home in the presence of the One who formed us.

Each of us brings our own preconceptions to the pursuit of God in our lives. Along with our hopes and longings, we often carry hurts and frustrations, misunderstandings and disappointments. This book offers the opportunity to make a fresh beginning. It lays the groundwork for a personal journey that leads Godward, while suggesting ways to move beyond the barriers—whether they are physical, psychological, emotional, or logistical—that hold us back.

The book is framed in eight chapters, each focused on a single aspect of time alone with God. At the conclusion of each chapter, you'll find seven days of meditations, intended to encourage and inspire your daily time with God and to help you find personal significance in the focus of the chapter. In addition, there are Scripture references, each of which offers further insight and a divine perspective on the nature and character of God and on our potential in relation to God. Use the readings as preparation to speak your heart in the quiet presence of God. And always be ready to listen.

This book does not present a prescription for world peace or personal wealth. It does not promise the answer to questions about suffering or evil or the vagaries of the stock market. What it does provide is a daily discipline that throughout the ages has ushered people like you and me into a deep and lifelong conversation with God.

Please accept the pages that follow as the expression of one seeker's experience. For the limitations and weaknesses any book surely contains, I ask forgiveness from God and from you. For whatever help it gives, I offer thanks. A book is just a book. Only God can satisfy the hunger in our souls.

D.D.

March 1999

CHAPTER ONE

Beginnings

FIVE ESSENTIALS *for* SEEKING GOD

THERE ARE MORE THINGS IN HEAVEN AND EARTH, HORATIO," WROTE WILLIAM SHAKESPEARE IN *HAMLET,* "THAN ARE DREAMT OF IN YOUR PHILOSOPHY." FOR MANY OF US, THE SEARCH FOR GOD BEGINS WITH JUST THAT SENSE, AND IT BECOMES OUR FIRST GUIDE TOWARD THE DIVINE. AS A CHILD, I SPENT ENDLESS HOURS EXPLORING A WORLD THAT WAS VISIBLE TO ME ALONE. IN THE TALL MEADOW GRASS BEHIND OUR HOUSE, I ENTERED A LONG and winding labyrinth leading to secret chambers where treasures hid and terrors awaited. When I climbed the old copper beech, I found kingdoms on every branch, where living creatures, however small, were workers or soldiers, adventurers or renegades. Stretched out on the log spanning a forest stream, I launched a thousand boats and barges, ships and rafts, onto the stream's swift eddies and tiny rapids.

In those times and places full of magic, I was up to more than child's play. It was ultimately a child's discovery of the spiritual—of the invisible possibilities and realities that lie beyond and behind the visible. I was exploring the life we cannot quantify or prove. Under the surface appearance of the world around me, I sensed a deeper reality. Over time, I discovered a name for that deeper reality. My early explorations evolved into a soul's search for God.

It is my belief that we long for God because we were created to be connected to God. Without the connection, we feel unwhole, orphaned. When we try to fill the longing with anything less than God (and if God exists, what isn't?), we come away less than satisfied. A yearning the size and shape of God needs God to fill it.

For many of us the search draws its power as well from our desire for truth. We want to know right from wrong, light from darkness, good from bad. We want to put our limited experience and understanding into a larger context that makes sense of what we perceive. We need to know that our lives ultimately mean something.

Yet many of us are stymied when it comes to satisfying the needs we feel. This begs the question: Why?

I think the answer for some of us lies in our early forays into organized religion. For one reason or another, what we saw and heard failed to reach us at the time. In some cases, we came to identify God with a less than meaningful or satisfying experience. We rejected the idea of God, or gave up on the search, not because of God but because of the way other people presented God.

Others of us struggle with the search for God at least in part because in this superficial age given to splashy pleasures and quick fixes, we do not easily develop a knack for depth, nor are we encouraged to invest the energy it requires. When we struggle with soul pain, we turn first to the loudest voice, the latest fad in feeling good. If we're lucky, it relieves our discomfort for a while. But it's not a cure, because it doesn't touch what we really want and need.

Further, our search for God is affected by the mystique of the specialist. We observe the lives and works of "religious" people—theologians, monks, mystics, or rabbis—who express their own interactions with the Divine. What we see produces in us awe bordering on the worshipful—as though they have a special pipeline to God that we could never hope for. We forget that these people are not located on some other plane of creation, somewhere between us and the angels, with some built-in propensity for the spiritual that the average human being can never have. They earned their insight. They worked for it. Not by making themselves over in the image of a contemplative or a guru or a shaman but, rather, by seeking God—day after day, week after week. They talked to God in prayer, asking the hard questions, exposing the guilty secrets, and humbly requesting forgiveness, understanding, and faith. They immersed themselves in the Scriptures, and considered what these writings reveal about life, human nature, and the Creator of both. And they took a sort of spiritual time-out, listening for the still, small voice—day after day, week after week. They allowed God time and space to work on them, even when they didn't feel like it, even when there were other demands that had to wait, even when God seemed far away.

Finally, we struggle with the very idea of connecting with God because we're so used to focusing on the *material* part of life; we're *comfortable* with what we can quantify and prove. Because God is spirit, in contrast to the material world, we are tempted to overspiritualize our part of any relationship with God. But for the many people of faith who have put a connection with God first in their lives, the seeking turns out to be only as spiritual as a human is capable of—good news indeed!—and it's grounded firmly in the stuff of discipline and choice.

Just as when we hope for a human relationship and want to make it as significant and true as possible, so too when we seek a relationship with God: There are specific choices we can make, particular habits we can adopt, attitudes we can foster. We need only the will to begin and the perseverance to keep at it.

Keys to Beginning

LET'S START BY POSITING THE TRUTH THAT GOD is not an idea but a personality, capable of knowing and being known by the whole created order. And God created us as the relational beings we are, meant to forge links with other people, with the rest of creation, and with our Maker. We know by observation and experience that no meaningful human relationship comes free of charge. There are essential elements to forming and growing a relationship. In their absence, the relationship never gets off the ground. Or if these elements are neglected in an established relationship, it eventually disintegrates. Often, the problems that send a couple, say, or siblings or an entire family into therapy are only the symptoms. The real problem is prior neglect; the essentials for health and growth have not been attended to, and trouble has inevitably followed.

What we experience with other people, we experience with God as well. It has to do with the way we as humans are put together. If we're serious about seeking God, we have to invest in the same key ele-

The Keys

TIME

SPACE

HUNGER

OPENNESS

COMMITMENT

ments that make any connection possible: time and space for the other; a cultivated hunger for that other that keeps us coming back; an openness that allows not only take but give as well; and a commitment to continue in the face of obstacles. Relating to God has its unique features, to be sure, and we'll get into those later, but they don't take away from the need for the essentials common to all relation-

ships. I find it comforting that God surely knows our needs and our limits in the relationship department. It gives me confidence to do what I'm capable of and leave the rest to God.

THE FIRST KEY *Time*

There's no substitute for giving time to a relationship. I made a best friend in first grade who remained with me all through school and beyond. For years, a day wasn't complete until we had put our heads together and talked out all that was on our minds. Nobody on earth knew me as Nancy did, and I knew her as though she were another me. We understood each other. We trusted each other. We depended on each other.

Then came further education, careers, and families. We ended up on opposite coasts, with only infrequent cards and letters and even more infrequent visits. Our reunions were miracles of laughter and rapport. We slipped into a mutual ease as though no time had passed. But, in fact, we were not current friends anymore. Our togetherness was based entirely on past history, and necessarily remote and disconnected. Not only had we missed the benefits of active friendship over miles and years, we had missed huge portions of each other's experiences, joys, sorrows, and growth. We no longer knew each other. We soon discovered that there were significant ways in which we didn't understand each other. We could no longer see from one another's point of view.

I consider this experience an apt, if limited, analogy for the spiritual realities of seeking God. I've heard people express their longing, especially in times of crisis, for a fuller spiritual life and specifically for a closer relationship with God. They want to understand what their lives mean in a "bigger picture." They have doubts and fears for which they can't find sufficient answers. They need greater wisdom, strength, compassion, patience—in their jobs, families, life choices. They harbor terrific anxieties about the death of those they love and of themselves. They've prayed on occasion, but when they don't see God's answer, they give it up. They hope for more, yet they don't set aside the time to pursue the relationship with God they claim to want. And they blame God for it.

Yet if any message can be culled consistently from the many voices of God seekers, including the writers of the Bible, it is this: The same God who created us as relation-oriented beings with a God-shaped need wants and intends to relate to us. In the 14th century, Lady Julian of Norwich expressed it this way: "Our inborn will is to have God, and the goodwill of God is to have us. . . . The love that God most high has for our soul is so great that it surpasses understanding." In other words, when it comes to difficulties with finding time for God, God is not the problem.

The question arises then: Why can't we find the time to seek God? I'll stick my neck out here to say that to need (or want) a more authentic spiritual life and then claim that you have no time for it is about as meaningful as to say you want to get married but don't have time to meet and date people. If I want a lifelong mate in my future, I will have to give the dating and courting phases the time they require. Those who choose not to do so will be understandably disappointed and lonely.

God doesn't need our conscious involvement to know and understand us, because God is God. But we need to consciously devote time to seeking God if we ever hope to enter into communication—even communion—with God. We don't know how long our journey from birth to death in this present life will be. We can only fuel up for the day, spiritually speaking, day after day, week after week.

How much time does it take? The answer to that changes from one day to the next, from one season of life to another. Sometimes, the more time we give to seeking God's company, the more we want. We discover that we've planted seeds, so to speak, and by keeping up and developing the practice of time with God, the seeds grow and bloom and give us the spiritual equivalent of wholesome food, beautiful flowers, and healing herbs. At other times, we can barely manage a 15-minute bubble before the day bursts in on us. But please notice that even the short times yield more than no time. And the longer times bring us to surprising insights and convictions. I think of a yoga instructor who routinely reminds her students that "little practice gives little benefit." Notice that she doesn't say "little" gives "no" benefit. But you get what you pay for, often in equal measure.

If you're having trouble thinking of any time you can regularly carve out for God, start with something simple.

- *Set the alarm a quarter or half hour earlier than usual.*
- *Save all or part of the morning paper to read at lunchtime.*
- *Skip the daily crossword puzzle.*
- *Eliminate an evening TV show.*
- *Institute a midafternoon break.*
- *Take spiritual advantage of the time that is freed up while a young child is napping, the clothes are washing, or dinner is simmering.*

Finding time for God may mean eliminating any one of a number of time wasters that we all accumulate along the way or limiting the time we spend on pursuits that mean relatively less to us. Within certain parameters—biological needs, job requirements, home duties—we can choose how we use our time. We simply forget sometimes that the choices are ours to make.

What we cannot dispense with, if we're serious about entering God's presence, is the *routine* of time to seek it, whatever the duration. If we depend on "feeling like it" or finding the time "somehow," it won't happen. If you want it to happen, you make it happen.

THE SECOND KEY *Space*

Space is a word, not unlike the word *spiritual,* that has taken on many shades of meaning in modern usage. There's physical space, of course, and, in fact, people throughout the ages have found or created physical spaces that they set apart specifically for time with God: a chapel, prayer room, or synagogue; a quiet corner; a particular chair or table; even a spot outdoors. These spaces allow for solitude of the soul. They help to engender a frame of mind. They contribute to our ability to focus, to leave unrelated thoughts and distractions behind for a period of time. Simply making the decision to designate such a space can help us to approach God regularly.

I'm not suggesting, however, that each of us needs to own one physical piece of "holy" ground in order to seek God's presence. People have made space for God in prison camps and foxholes, tenements, locker rooms, and lunar modules. Much more to the point is the psychological space we create. It involves an active decision to limit distractions, to short-circuit potential interruptions, and to consciously put aside preoccupations. In this way, we ourselves become holy ground.

Making Space for God

IDENTIFY DISTRACTIONS

CONTROL INTERRUPTIONS

PUT PREOCCUPATIONS IN THEIR PLACE

Consider the space robbers—distractions, interruptions, and preoccupations—in more detail.

Distractions are those elements in your life that "call" you when you're otherwise engaged.

I remember a writer-colleague of mine who claimed that every writing project led to a minimum 5-pound gain in weight. It never failed that in the midst of a writing spell, she would find herself beckoned away from the keyboard by whatever sweet concoction happened to be at hand. It wasn't until she found a reliably quiet nook at the local library—no food allowed—where she could set up her laptop computer that she got the distraction (and her weight) under control. It seems to be one of life's little psychological ironies that we are most easily diverted when engaged in what matters most to us. For whatever reason—whether it's fear of what will come out of our endeavors (or what will not), laziness, or simply a short attention span—we often need to work the hardest to stay with the disciplines that will do us the most good. This is no less true in regard to time with God.

⚜ *The first step to taking control of distractions is to identify them.* Every individual is different. Depending on where and when you make time and space for God, your nemesis may be the dirty laundry, a list of phone messages, the unwashed car, the Internet, the answering machine, or a great half-read novel. Pay attention to the moments when your attention strays, and you'll be able to name your own personal coterie of distractions.

⚜ *The next step is to make the changes that keep identified distractions at bay.* You may find that you need to be out of sight of regular chores, even by so simple a choice as turning a chair so that all you see is the view out a window (unless, of course, the view itself is a distraction). You may have to avoid times that are too heavily associated with other activities (mealtime doesn't tend to be a good choice—eat first). You may even have to reconsider some old habits. Terry used to routinely listen to *Morning Pro Musica* on public radio at what became his best option for time alone with God. As good as it was, the program was not an accompaniment conducive to meditation or prayer. Until Terry found an alternative time for God (as he did a few years later), he decided he could do without *Morning Pro Musica*. What he gained, Terry felt, far outweighed his loss.

Interruptions are the active intrusions on our solitude that steal moments of quality and concentration.

These may be easier to identify than the more subtle distractions, in part because many of them have human faces. Whether family members, friends, solicitors, delivery people, or a ringing telephone, they all share the distinction of stopping us in the middle of something solitary to demand attention.

Dealing productively with interruptions often requires a bit of diplomacy and a spirit of collaboration. At heart, it involves establishing your right to time and place alone, especially in your own thinking. History, biblical and otherwise, is full of examples of people who made their need for solitude with God clear to those around them and subsequently reaped the benefits from it. The more congenially you can do this, of course, the more likely you are to have cooperation. For example:

✺ *Treat your solitary time as you would an important business appointment.* When friends or extended family want to preempt your time, you can simply say, "I'm sorry. I'm not available then." You don't have to explain if you don't want to. You can legitimately call it an appointment if that makes it easier.

🌿 *For immediate family, you may have to negotiate.* When my children were young, I found that the only time I could rescue from the real demands of children and husband was before dawn. At the time, I was the only early riser in the group. A former student tells me that the time during which other family members are watching prime-time TV gives him the freedom to be alone.

🌿 *You may have to trade time with other adult or young adult family members.* "Give me this hour free, and I'll safeguard that hour for you." It's fair play, and everyone benefits.

🌿 *You may find it helpful to take yourself out of reach.* Some folks find it difficult, even with the best intentions, to leave a quiet person alone. If you aren't there, you can't be interrupted.

🌿 *If your problem is a ringing phone, do yourself a quick and easy favor.* Take it off the hook. Anyone calling about emergencies and important business will try again later.

Preoccupations—the nagging sirens of our thought life— are perhaps the trickiest to deal with.

They erupt when we least want or need them (mine are partial to the middle of the night), and they steal both our focus and our peace. As with distractions, the first step to defusing preoccupations is to recognize them when they come calling. They take the form of worries or anxieties, to-do items that need remembering, frustrations or hurts, or unresolved problems. They all loom large when we're in a vulnerable frame of mind, tired, or clearing our thoughts of other business. Sometimes, there's nothing we can do about them, no matter how much attention we give them. Almost invariably, they can at least be deferred for an hour or so. But if we let them, they crowd out reflection, meditation, and prayer.

Dealing with preoccupations demands some level of what I call self-talk. By that I mean that we acknowledge them, then firmly put them in their place. In essence, we say, "Yes, you're a concern, all right. But I'm not dealing with you right now. You'll have to wait your turn." Clearing preoccupations from the space we've reserved for God may be as simple as keeping a small pad of paper, a pen, and an envelope close at hand. When you find yourself being pulled away from a God-centered frame of mind—whether by a worry, something you need to remember, or even some great solution to a problem—quickly write down whatever thought is tugging at you and put the paper it's written on in the envelope. Doing this gets the thought both off your mind and out of sight. Use this tactic as often as need be. In time, you may find you can do it without the paper and pen. The heart of dealing with preoccupations is finding some place to put them so they cannot fill the space saved for God. It helps me always to keep in the back of my mind that preoccupations are ready and able to subvert me—but only if I allow them to do so.

THE THIRD KEY *Hunger*

A doctor once told me not to worry about my children's eating preferences. He said to give them a wide variety of choices and let their appetites dictate what and how much they ate. Their bodies, he said, would demand what they needed. Over time, they would want what produced health.

In theory, he spoke the truth. What I quickly discovered, however, was that this method only worked when every element among the options was wholesome. Given the choice between broccoli and a gummy bear, my children invariably chose the candy.

To create and continue the practice of time with God, we need a spiritual appetite that hungers for God's presence. The world we live in feeds us a constant supply of spiritual junk food. We can easily fill our time with TV, videos, surfing the Net, and cruising the malls. For every book of substance that appears, a dozen more crop up that offer little more than a short spell of escape from our routine. Because our culture is preoccupied with appearances, we devote ourselves to excessive dieting and exercise, tanning booths, nail jobs, plastic surgery, and beauty treatments. We've taken professional and college sports to the point of mass hysteria, and we're taught to worship at the shrine of human achievement—as if celebrities and billionaires were the highest possible expression of human hopes.

The insidious thing about junk food is that it eventually distorts our appetite. This is true of the literal food we eat, as evidenced by the fattening of modern societies in which junk food has taken over the shelves of the supermarkets. And it's true of spiritual food. The more junk we take in, the more we want and the less of an appetite we have for that which will truly nourish our souls.

To nurture our hunger for God's presence, we need to retrain our appetites by spending time with God even if we don't hunger for it. The experience will itself sharpen our spiritual appetite.

THE FOURTH KEY *Openness*

If time with God has as its focus a growing connectedness—a relationship—then an open spirit becomes indispensable. We sometimes enter into a give-and-take with the unacknowledged need to establish ourselves more thoroughly in our own point of view. Yet any true conversation demands two-way communication, and communication cannot travel in two directions unless we are open to hear a voice different from our own. In Martin Buber's terms, "the I–You relation entails a reciprocity that embraces both the I and the You." We have to acknowledge the legitimacy of the other in order to allow that other a share in the dialogue. Specifically, consider three types of openness: hearing God, accepting change, and being surprised.

We will stunt the potential of a transcendent conversation unless we open ourselves to listen— that is, to hear God.

When we seek the presence of God, we often begin with talk. To listen instead may mean silencing our own fears or persuasions. It may mean laying aside our presuppositions, insofar as we're able. It will without a doubt require that at some point we stop talking. Only in the quiet that ensues will we clear the air for the voice of God.

How do we hear God's voice?

- *God speaks to us in the nudges of what we call conscience.*
- *God speaks through the words of Scripture.*
- *Sometimes we hear God's voice in the advice and comfort of other people or in the beauty of nature or art.*
- *We hear the voice of God in the literature of the ages.*
- *We hear God in moments of great mental or emotional clarity.*
- *Some even hear God in dreams or visions.*

People who have been successful in making time with God an integral part of their daily lives all describe the same basic effect: The more time they devote to God, the clearer the voice of God becomes in reference to their lives.

Of course, it is possible to feel our own urges and inclinations and believe they are God's voice. In that case, the essential problem resides in what I call pseudo-listening, the polar opposite of openness. It comes from something akin to praying in an echo chamber. My own voice is both questioner and answerer, by which I effectively drown God out.

When we reject the echo-chamber phenomenon, we make possible a second kind of openness essential to time with God, openness to change.

It can be frightening to imagine that we will personally experience the presence of the Divine and we will be changed. That's why we often hug our attitudes and our preconceptions, even our weaknesses, and certainly our ignorance around us like well-loved garments that we refuse to part with. Our time with God becomes dominated by ego and self-protection. In that case, why bother to spend time with God?

If an unwillingness to listen for God is like an echo-chamber conversation, an unwillingness to change is like praying to a mirror.

In contrast, imagine yourself completely exposed and open to the transformative power of the One who made you, who knows you best, and who knows what is best both in you and for you. We bring the fears that our experiences with people have taught us. The essential ingredient to opening ourselves to change is trust in the Changer. And the corollary to trust is courage. Change tends to scare us, yet it is the

Three Types
of Openness

HEARING GOD

ACCEPTING CHANGE

BEING SURPRISED

most promising and exciting of all human adventures, and where it does not exist, life itself ceases. Rather than resisting or running from change, why not open ourselves to it in the ultimate venue—the presence of God?

Once we entertain the possibility of change, we more readily open ourselves to be surprised.

Think for a moment of the simple perceptual exercise of looking at an optical illusion—for instance, a picture in two solid colors that seen in one way looks like a vase and in another way looks like two profiles facing each other. If we are predisposed to see one of the images, we can easily miss the other entirely. This is no less true with God. How very sad to miss a great revelation, a miraculous healing, or a new possibility offered in full and glorious color simply because we allowed our expectations to define what we would hear or experience or understand.

Just consider what we have learned about the workings of the universe, from the infinitesimal to the infinite, in all their wondrous diversity and balance and beauty, and then imagine the scope and depth and mystery of the One who brought all that exists into being. In the natural world alone, we never run out of new avenues to explore. I would far rather open myself to the full range of divine surprises than limit myself to what I can imagine or expect.

THE FINAL KEY *Commitment*

In the long run, every worthwhile endeavor requires one indispensable element, and that is our commitment. Whether it's an important relationship to build and maintain, a job to do, a contract to fulfill, or a responsibility to carry out, it ultimately stands or falls on our commitment to start, to continue, and to see it through to the end. Good intentions and promises finally mean nothing until we commit ourselves to do and keep doing. It is a choice.

In the case of time alone with God, we have just as certain a need to commit ourselves. It is a discipline that calls on self-control, priorities, imagination, and faithfulness.

There will be times, without a doubt, when we're frustrated. We can take some of the power out of the frustrations, however, by expecting them. Know ahead of time—and I promise you it's true—that emergencies *will* arise to steal the time you have reserved for God. You will encounter unavoidable distractions and interruptions. Preoccupations will periodically, temporarily overwhelm you. Furthermore, you will experience a loss of hunger for God's presence from time to time. Periods of depression, anger, confusion, or grief may get in your way, leaving you tired and unwilling to seek God (more about this later). In any case, the surest cure is to give yourself the benefit of the doubt.

If you tend to be a perfectionist, cut yourself some slack. Humbly admit that you are not perfect, accept the times when you don't do what you intend, and start again.

If you're frightened, angry, or overwhelmed, bring those feelings to your time with God. That's the place where you can feel what you feel with confidence because you are in the presence of Someone who already knows. God will be neither shocked nor disappointed. According to Scripture, the only way we ultimately disappoint God is by refusing to seek God.

If you are carrying a load of guilt about something, take courage. To avoid God in such a time is to avoid the only One in the universe who finally has the right or the wisdom to judge and who also has the power to forgive. Where *better* to carry the burden of guilt than into the presence of God?

In the final analysis, commitment means that no matter how many setbacks we encounter, no matter how great the temptation is to give in to other urgencies, we keep coming back to time with God. In this discipline, we begin the greatest exploration available to humankind and the most significant personal relationship we will ever experience.

Meditations

ON BEGINNING

On the next several pages you will find some thoughts and suggested Bible readings meant to encourage you in your time alone with God. You may find it helpful to put in writing how you intend to spend time alone with God in the coming week— the time, the place, the circumstances. Try to be as realistic and specific as possible. It may be better to start small and grow rather than overestimate what you can do and then feel that you've let yourself down. However you proceed, let these meditations be a launching point or an inspiration, a guide or simply a shared moment with another seeker.

Day One

"There is a time for everything," states the writer of Ecclesiastes in chapter 3, verse 1, "and a season for every activity under heaven." How often do we declare, "There's no time!" about some activity or relationship that we're trying to "fit in."

In fact, our time is limited, but not necessarily in the way we think. It's true that we've been given only so many days in this present existence. But each and every one of them is a gift from God and carries with it a day's worth of obligations and opportunities, anticipations and worries, joys and sorrows. We have the option to make new choices every day about how we will use our time. We can rethink past decisions. We can invent new possibilities. We can redeem old ones.

How do you choose to use God's gift of time today?

BIBLE READINGS

Ecclesiastes 8:6-8   Matthew 6:25-27

Day Two

In *The Wounded Healer,* Henri Nouwen wrote, "When we are not afraid to enter into our own center and to concentrate on the stirrings of our own soul, we come to know that being alive means being loved." *When we are not afraid* . . . Fear has its place in the preservation of life. It can give us the strength to defend ourselves and those we love, and it can give us the stamina to flee to safety when we're threatened. But fear can also become a habit that sends us running or raises our defenses in the wrong times and circumstances.

When we seek God, the only fear we need feel is reverent awe as mortal beings in the presence of our Immortal Maker.

What fears do you harbor that make you want to keep your distance from God?

BIBLE READINGS

Psalm 25:12-15   Matthew 14: 22-32

Day Three

"Superficiality is the curse of our age," writes Richard J. Foster in *Celebration of Discipline.* "The doctrine of instant satisfaction is a primary spiritual problem." We are pelted with constant messages that there are quick and easy solutions to all problems, fast tracks to any goal.

Yet in the realm of the soul, patience can keep us from abandoning the space we have cleared for God.

What of great value in your life have you had to wait for? What are you willing to wait for before God?

BIBLE READINGS

Isaiah 30:18   Colossians 1:9-14

Day Four

An increasing number of researchers, nutritionists, and psychologists say that we often keep eating, despite the amount that we've ingested, because the food we've ingested hasn't provided the nutrients our bodies need and crave.

So, too, in the spiritual realm. We have real spiritual needs that create palpable spiritual hunger. Our search for satisfaction becomes desperate—sometimes even destructive—unless we are finding real nourishment for our souls.

In what part of your life do you experience your greatest hunger?

BIBLE READINGS

Psalm 42:1-11   John 4:9-14

Day Five

A closed hand can receive no gift.

A closed mouth can receive no food.

A closed wound can receive no cleansing.

A closed heart can receive no love.

In the stillness of God's presence, search out what is closed in your spirit today. Even the slightest opening can let in God's grace and sustenance, forgiveness and love.

What makes it most difficult for you to open your soul to the presence of God?

BIBLE READINGS

Psalm 139:7-14   *Matthew 11:25-30*

Day Six

*D*o the explanations people have made about God get in the way of who and what God may really be to us? Most of us want to explain and prove. We want to create logical, linear reasonings that wrap up all that we experience in neat packages.

"God cannot be expressed," writes Frederick Buechner in *Wishful Thinking*, "but only experienced."

Do we shy away from a soul-deep experience with God because we haven't been able to find a way to "express" God in a logical, understandable package?

What do you find most challenging about the mystery of God? How can your powers of reasoning serve you as you seek God's mysterious presence?

BIBLE READINGS

Job 42:1-5   Hebrews 11:1-2

Day Seven

"Whether it be shallow or not," writes Scott Peck in *The Road Less Traveled*, "commitment is the foundation, the bedrock of any genuinely loving relationship."

When we make a commitment, we pledge something. In the case of a relationship with God, we begin by pledging some of our time, our attention, our consideration. If we stop there, we may gain some insight and earn some quiet, but we will limit the relationship.

If time alone with God is truly to foster the growth of our relationship with God, one commitment must develop into other, deeper commitments. We move from pledging our time and attention to pledging our actions and our attitudes, and eventually—if we really hope to fill the God-size need in the soul—ourselves.

In seeking time alone with God, what commitment will you make today?

BIBLE READINGS

Psalm 37:3-6   *Romans 12:1-2*

O God, you are my God,
    earnestly I seek you;
my soul thirsts for you,
    my body longs for you,
in a dry and weary land
    where there is no water.

I have seen you in the sanctuary
    and beheld your power
    and your glory.
Because your love is better than life,
    my lips will glorify you.
I will praise you as long as I live,
    and in your name
    I will lift up my hands.
My soul will be satisfied
    as with the richest of foods;
    with singing lips
    my mouth will praise you.

Psalm 63:1–5

CHAPTER TWO

Who Am I?

FACES *of the* SINCERE SEEKER

EARLY IN THE 17TH CENTURY, GALILEO GALILEI OFFERED PROOF THAT THE HERETICAL THEORIES OF AN EARLIER SCIENTIST NAMED NICOLAUS COPERNICUS WERE IN FACT TRUE. THE EARTH, PROCLAIMED GALILEO, WAS NOT THE CENTER OF THE UNIVERSE, WITH SUN, MOON, STARS, AND PLANETS ORBITING AROUND IT. RATHER, IT WAS THE SUN AT THE CENTER AROUND WHICH EVERYTHING REVOLVED, INCLUDING THE EARTH AND ITS satellite moon. With the Copernican theories before him, Galileo had set out to discover the truth, and with all the energy of a determined seeker, he eventually developed a telescope powerful enough to provide solid evidence that his own theories were sound.

Human history is a millennia-long saga of seekers such as Galileo. Who sent us around our globe, to the ocean floors, and beyond Earth's atmosphere into space if not the seekers? Seekers have shaken off the chains of slavery. They've built empires. And they've discovered galaxies. Perhaps best of all, they've chased the dream of a great love or an elusive cure. The seeking spirit in us has inspired our greatest works of art and our most courageous acts. And it has impelled us toward God.

We begin our adventure toward God by making time and space for God, by cultivating our appetite for God's presence and opening ourselves to it, and by committing ourselves to continuing the pursuit of a connection with God. These are choices, and they have to be made again and again if we hope to keep the practice of time with God alive, honest, and meaningful.

At the same time, we find the wellspring of motivation and energy to make these choices from within our seeking spirit—that which reaches out from us to God. If we recognize and nurture the various aspects, or what I will call faces, of that spirit, we can tap at will the source that reinforces our motivation and feeds our energy for the great enterprise ahead.

The Faces of a Seeker

CHARLIE, AN ARDENT GARDENER FRIEND OF mine, moved from our region of verdant springs and lush summers, where he knew the flora and understood its requirements, to a hot, dry area. He had the heart of a gardener. He longed to create a garden with the beauty and color he loved. So he arranged his new life to allow the time and resources to seek what he missed.

Charlie's garden did not shape up quickly or easily. He found a variety of familiar plants and carefully prepared the ground for them, fed them, and watered them. And season after season his lovely shrub and flower beds languished. His letters became dirgelike over time as his failed experiments with different plantings mounted up. Yet he would not give up. He believed that the earth—even the sere land of his new home—could and would yield beauty. He was convinced that it was his own limitations of knowledge and experience that prevented his efforts from succeeding. And so his love of growing things drove him forward to try again and again.

Then one bright winter morning, the first after many days of the region's short rainy season, a friend came by and invited Charlie to drive out into the desert with her. As they left suburbia and headed into the usually desolate hills, Charlie was flabbergasted to see a spectacular display of natural color. The desert had come alive with blossoms. Within weeks, Charlie had examined many of the remarkable plants blooming in the desert and had begun a catalog of their names and requirements. In the subsequent planting seasons, he developed a garden that suited both the region and his desire for color and form. In time, it became a showplace that drew many visitors.

Charlie in the garden paints a wonderful picture of the sincere seeker in the presence of God. He is first and foremost a *believer.* He believes that the earth in all its variety is alive and that life can be cultivated from it. He is also, when faced with the mysteries and challenges of nature, a *child.* As he entered into the challenge of creating beauty in a desert, he acknowledged his own limitations and his need to learn and grow. He understood his dependence on forces outside his control, and he treated them with respect. And he is a *lover.* No amount of frustration or failure can kill his passion for the garden. With each setback, he simply becomes more determined to find a way to make it work.

Faces of the Seeker

THE BELIEVER

THE CHILD

THE LOVER

Every sincere seeker wears these faces—the believer, the child, the lover—to some degree. Behind them lie attitudes that keep us learning, growing, and finding new resources within ourselves. This is especially true as we seek the presence of God. Such a search is not some dry ritual or intellectual exercise but, rather, the pursuit of a living, challenging relationship with the Divine. The state of heart and mind we bring to the search plays a critical role in how far the search will take us. As we discover our seeking faces, we can allow them to blossom in the presence of God.

FACE OF THE BELIEVER *A Single Focus*

I will never forget the moment when one of my college professors stood before us, his students, and declared with intensity, "God save us all from true believers!"

I was taken aback. Of all the teachers—or students, for that matter—I had encountered at school, this particular man seemed to hold the strongest convictions about nearly everything. I could easily have labeled him a true believer himself. Because his happened to be a philosophy class, such a declaration could hardly go undiscussed— in fact, he intended to lure us into discussion. But in the course of our conversation, it came out that the professor had suffered a close encounter with a Ku Klux Klan rally that had demonstrated for him some of the worst and most frightening potentials of "true belief."

The lesson I took from the class was simply this: Belief is a power to be reckoned with, and its potential for good or bad is directly related to the object of belief. Belief in an idea or ideology that is fundamentally flawed can produce great harm. Belief in the living God, as we act it out in a sincere search for God's presence in our lives, can tap into the greatest imaginable power for good. If we focus our belief singularly on the Originator of good, we put ourselves in the path of that power.

Priest and teacher Henri Nouwen once wrote: "To say with all that we have, think, feel, and are, 'God exists' is the most world-shattering statement that a human being can make. . . . When we say this from the heart, everything trembles in heaven and on earth. Because when God exists, all that *is* flows from God."

Nouwen describes here a fundamental characteristic of belief, equally true for the explorer, the scientist, the conqueror, the abolitionist, or the God seeker: *Belief changes the way we view the universe.* It seems to me that all history's movers and shakers started with at least a grain of belief, *then* discovered, proved, vanquished, emancipated, connected to God—in fact, changed their world and, in some cases, the future of the human race. Galileo and those before him were taught by the thinkers and theologians of their time to understand the heavens as an Earth-centered system. They had to harbor at least the seed of belief in a different reality to take the first step toward discovering the truth.

For the one who sincerely seeks God's presence, belief is also the first step. The writer of Hebrews in the Christian Bible gives a long list of people whose search was answered by God, and the one quality all these people shared was *belief*—not perfect morality, not exceptional holiness or noble character, but belief. They were a motley collection that included liars, adulterers, thieves, and murderers. Yet they responded to their belief in God by reaching in God's direction, and God met them. In the process, the believers came to a new vision of God, of themselves, and of the relationship between them.

Sometimes we carry the seed of belief in us without recognizing it. I remember Janet, a seminar attendee who arrived at class one evening in an agitated state. "I want to believe," she told us. "But I don't know what it *means* to believe."

As the group worked together to address Janet's concern, various individuals began to talk about the characteristics of their own belief. As I listened to the wide–ranging descriptions that followed, it occurred to me that many of us, like Janet, have a core of God-centered belief that we have never learned how to draw on as we seek God.

Like the wind, which we see indirectly by what it does, so belief becomes visible to us through the attitudes it produces in us. In turn, the attitudes become the ground on which God meets us in our search. Consider some examples.

Belief

A SOURCE OF AWE

INSPIRATION FOR THANKSGIVING

THE DOOR TO HONESTY

FREEDOM TO DEAL WITH REGRETS

✤ *To believe in God produces awe in us.* Awe is the reverent fear that grows in us as we pay attention to the majesty and beauty, the balance and intricacy, of creation. It is awe that helps us acknowledge that we are creatures seeking our Creator. The very act of searching out the wondrous in creation teaches us to know God better, and our belief blossoms. So too does awe grow as we reflect on Scripture, in which God reveals the divine perspective on our lives.

    ✒ *Belief inspires thanksgiving for life as a gift full of potential from God.* A gift offers little meaning or benefit to us until we accept it. Every time we gratefully recognize the gift of life and all that it holds and promises for us, we in effect open ourselves to the full measure of what God can bring about in our lives.

    ✒ *Belief opens the door to honesty.* God already knows all about us; there's nothing we can or should hide. In God's presence, we are safe to search out more of who and what we are, to put ourselves in God's keeping, and to let self-knowledge lead to growth. At the same time, we come to desire a closer experience with God that will make that growth reach new levels.

    ✒ *Belief frees us to deal with our regrets in repentance.* Repentance refers to a moral change in direction. Sometimes self-discovery in God's presence brings to light actions and attitudes that we long to have forgiven and leave behind us. As we turn to God in belief, we make the primary turning from attitudes and actions that take us away from God. Over time, we learn to recognize—and regret—what separates us from God, and this makes us willing to change.

    Kathleen Norris, in *Amazing Grace,* points out that the Greek root of the verb *to believe* means "to give your heart to." Belief has the power to give our spirit a single, miraculous focus—God.

FACE OF THE CHILD *A Single Self*

It always makes me sad to find a parent or mentor trying to rush a child into adulthood. When I see a child loaded down with competitive activities or pushed into accelerated education or dressed in sophisticated, "grown-up" styles, a voice inside me cries, "Wait! That'll come all too soon! Savor the child!" I saw a photograph not long ago of two children running barefoot up a meadow hill. The children's backs were to the camera, but I didn't need to see their faces to sense their exuberance and freedom. I remember thinking, "If only I could bottle what they have!" In fact, they seemed to capture the essence of the simpler spirit we can enjoy in the presence of God.

There is something wondrous about a child, a quality that wise people throughout the ages have cherished and pointed to when they considered what is best and most hopeful in humankind. As the ancient Chinese philosopher Mencius declared more than two thousand years ago, "The great man is one who does not lose his child's heart." The child's heart is another face of the seeker's heart.

What is our "child's heart," and what makes it so central to our search for God's presence in our lives?

The gospel writer Matthew tells a story of when Jesus of Nazareth's followers came to him and asked, "Who is the greatest in the kingdom of heaven?" Jesus responded by calling a small child into their company and saying, "Unless you become like little children, you will never enter the kingdom of heaven." What made that child especially fit for the "kingdom of heaven"—that is, for the presence of God? As I reflect on some of the characteristics of childlikeness, I see some of the most important traits for a life that can be transformed by the power and love of the Almighty.

For starters, children recognize their dependence. Small children have no resources with which to care and provide for themselves, too little experience and strength and power. They are literally at the mercy of the adults and external forces in their lives—utterly dependent—and whether they know what to call it or not, they feel their vulnerability. As adults, we sometimes lose sight of how dependent we continue to be. We forget how much is out of our control, how much we do not know, how quickly and thoroughly all that we have and do can be lost. When we retain or reclaim our "child's heart," we recognize our dependence. And as seekers, we look not to other adults but to God.

Children are teachable. One of my most enjoyable experiences in a classroom was teaching kindergarten. To the children, something as ordinary as the alphabet was a wonderful adventure, and they nearly jumped out of their seats when they mastered the printing of their own names. No sooner did they make one discovery than they were bounding forward to the next. They were like laughing, dancing little sponges. As adults, our caution or skepticism often prevents us from seizing the opportunity to be taught, even by God, and consequently from experiencing the exuberance of learning.

    ✿ *Children embody a spirit of simplicity.* Some years ago, I got to know a woman who had great difficulty relating to other adults, especially in social situations. Yet invariably, if children were present, I would find her right in the midst of them. We called her the Pied Piper because by the end of any social event, she would have a trail of children happily following her around. I once asked her why she felt so much more comfortable with the children.

    "Because what you see is what you get," she replied. "A child doesn't say, 'I'm a doctor' or 'I just bought a new house' or 'I have a great deal you might want to get in on.' A child simply *is*, for better or worse." Instead of job titles, status symbols, or ambitious agendas, children bring with them a sense of fun, curiosity, and imagination.

    Imagine bringing only yourself to God—no things (or cravings for them), no elaborate plans (other than spending time alone with God), and no program (or list of items to accomplish). What a freeing encounter that would be, and how different from nearly every human interaction we engage in.

    ✿ *Children are malleable.* It is in the nature of childhood that children have a spirit that readily grows and changes. Our adult belongings

Childlikeness

RECOGNITION OF
DEPENDENCE

TEACHABILITY

THE SPIRIT OF
SIMPLICITY

MALLEABILITY

and desires, goals and preconceptions, often box us into a way of thinking and living. Time alone with God cannot shape us or turn us in new directions if we arrive in a closed box and never venture out. The sincere seeker who wears the face of the child has at least opened the lid of the box, if not climbed out altogether.

Our spirit finds a simpler resting place when, with the face of a child, we bring a single, unencumbered self into the presence of God.

FACE OF THE LOVER *A Single Heart*

There is perhaps no theme that so inspires and engages our imagination as that of passionate human love. It infuses our thinking, philosophy, literature, theater, entertainment, and arts. It is the sharpest edge of many joys and sorrows, raising us to heights and plunging us to depths. Even the Bible includes a book, the Song of Songs (also called the Song of Solomon), that draws its imagery mainly from the vocabulary and experience of human lovers.

We tend to divorce our experience of human love from the love that is toward and from God. Yet I'm greatly drawn to the idea put forward by the 18th–century theologian Jonathan Edwards. Edwards suggested that all the "things of the world" are simultaneously images of the Divine. In other words, human love can be a picture, however limited or flawed, of our love for and from God.

We can lay this picture alongside what Scripture has to say about the relationship between God and people, spelled out in part in the Ten Commandments of the Bible. We sometimes view the Ten Commandments—which is a kind of divine blueprint for relationships—as a collection of burdensome negatives. In contrast, Moses summed up the commandments in this way: "Love the Lord your God with all your heart and with all your soul and with all your strength." Jesus declared that the first great commandment was "to love the Lord your God with all your heart and with all your soul and with all your mind and with all your strength." At the heart of the commandments then, we find love, and it's an all-encompassing love at that.

I believe that we often so spiritualize the idea of love between us and God that we forget what we've learned about love from one another. Yet we are not asked to love God only with all our soul and all our mind, but with all our heart and strength as well, and it is our experience of human love that gives a powerful and compelling reality to our love for God.

With the face of the believer, the sincere seeker brings a single focus to the pursuit of God; with the face of the child, the seeker brings a single self. But the lover in the seeker soars beyond these two, investing the search with an ardent spirit that won't take "no" for an answer. The psalmist used the language of a lover when he wrote this seeker's hymn: "As the deer pants for streams of water, so my soul pants for you, O God. My soul thirsts for God, for the living God. When can I go and meet God?" Such longing must be satisfied, he suggests, and the seeker will persevere wholeheartedly until it is.

It is God who created us with the potential for such all-encompassing passion. And this gift, perhaps above all others, has the power to transform our spirit. Consider the course of human love and what it reveals about love in the presence of God.

The first strong phase of love is the feeling of desire. We have an overwhelming longing for the company and attention of the loved one. We look forward to time together, grow forlorn when the time to part draws near, and pine for the other until reunion takes place. I have met numerous people of faith who after years of daily time with God could not happily neglect God for even a day. One friend said, "I feel physical pain when I can only snatch moments out of my day for God." Another has told me that God is "the love of my life."

When desire is answered in kind, we find ourselves "in love." Scott Peck, in *The Road Less Traveled,* describes this state as "the sudden release of oneself from oneself, the explosive pouring out of oneself into the beloved, and the dramatic surcease of loneliness." When we fall in love, we sometimes speak of a soul mate. We find someone who understands what we mean when we speak, feels the import of things that matter to us, appreciates the best in us, and forgives the worst. This phenomenon does not occur only between romantic lovers; it happens between parent and child, between friend and friend. And this state of love can exist between Creator and creature.

    ✺ *Such love leads to devotion, a dedicated connection to the other.* With it comes a sense of loyalty, a willingness to serve and please the other, not because we must but because we want to. In fact, nothing makes us happier than those opportunities when we can act out our love. And "devotion," of course, is what we call the practice of time alone with God in prayer and worship.

    ✺ *As we come to know that our devotion for another is mutual, we learn to trust.* Because we believe in the loving intentions of the one we love, we are prepared to make ourselves vulnerable. When we trust—that is, when we feel safe—we willingly give. We are freed to be who and what we are. And we are freed to take risks and change. It's hard to trust other people, in part because we know enough about the ways that we ourselves let other people down and we project our own failures onto them. When we seek God, we need to sort out the distrust we've learned in the company of people. God is not human and not subject to the frailties and failures of humankind. God can be trusted.

With the face of the lover, we put our heart into seeking God.

I don't mean finally to suggest that every sincere seeker has a precise and perfect mix of believer, child, and lover. We all start in our own way and proceed out of the unique combination of personality

Love

THE FEELING
OF DESIRE

THE STATE OF
BEING IN LOVE

DEVOTION TO
ANOTHER

THE ABILITY
TO TRUST

and circumstances that make us individuals. Beyond that, our seeking may be tinged with doubts or fears, anger or rebellion. But I do believe that without some measure of the believer, the child, and the lover, we will find our time with God a dry and rocky place—full of burdensome duties and lifeless propositions—instead of the passionate personal journey fueled by love that fills the mind, the heart, and the soul of the sincere seeker.

Meditations

ON THE SEEKER'S HEART

The following meditations are designed to further your reflections on the ideas presented in this chapter. Before you proceed, however, take the time to consider your recent time alone with God. Do you need to rethink your choices regarding time and place? Adjust how you approach your coming time with God in light of what you have experienced. Make a specific, realistic commitment for another week. Then allow your prayers and reflections to help you discover aspects of the sincere seeker that are growing in you.

Day One

How do we first walk on our own two feet? We start by putting one foot in front of the other by reflex, while a loving adult holds on to our hands. Later, we learn to take our own experimental steps while clinging to furniture. Eventually, we combine what we've experienced with what we believe—that if we let go of supports and put one foot in front of the other, we will walk without our legs giving out or our balance failing. It is a courageous act of faith.

We repeat some version of this process to read, to swim, to ride a bike, to make a friend, to build a house, or to create a nation. And we repeat it when we seek God. At some point, information and experience must be ignited by belief to learn and grow. Belief is not a state we enter once and for all. Belief is a daily action, and it grows along with us. Is there a new step of belief in God before you today?

BIBLE READINGS

Proverbs 14:26-27   Hebrews 11:6

Day Two

The Gospel writer Mark relates a story from the life of Jesus that gets to the essence of belief. A man—the father of a sick boy—brought his child to Jesus to be healed. "If you can do anything," the father added after he had made his request.

"'If you can?'" Jesus repeated, adding, "Everything is possible for him who believes."

Then the father offered one of the most profoundly honest declarations of faith ever recorded. "I do believe!" he exclaimed. "Help me overcome my unbelief."

God never asks that we pretend. In fact, God knows better and sooner than we do the condition of our faith. It is enough to say with the sick boy's father, "I believe. Help me overcome my unbelief."

BIBLE READINGS

Genesis 15:1-6   *Matthew 17:14-20*

Day Three

At the dedication of his corporation's Manhattan headquarters, James Cash (more commonly known as "J. C.") Penney commented, "I wouldn't be human if I didn't feel pride and something that transcends pride—humility." His pride was understandable. But what about the humility that "transcends pride"?

Perhaps at that high point in his life, Penney was acutely conscious of how much help he'd had along the way, from other people and from circumstances. Perhaps, too, he acknowledged that even his ability to achieve was a gift.

When we seek the presence of God, we can do no better than to assess ourselves honestly. It may humble us. But we then can allow God to be the One who raises us to a higher place—a far more secure height than any we could hope for without God's support. Are there ways today in which you need to see yourself more realistically before God?

BIBLE READINGS

2 Chronicles 7:11-14   *Matthew 18:1-4*

Day Four

Robert Frost once said, "There is the fear that we shan't prove worthy in the eyes of someone who knows us at least as well as we know ourselves. That is the fear of God."

Examine your own "fear of God." Ask yourself what you fear that God will not find worthy in you and why.

BIBLE READINGS

Psalm 139:1-4   *Hebrews 4:12-13*

Day Five

I have heard many stories about adopted children who eventually felt compelled to search for their biological parents. Their need did not necessarily grow from a bad experience with the parents who raised them. They simply longed for the faces and personalities, the legends and legacies, behind the bare facts of their adoption.

It is from our family line that we inherit much of what makes us who and what we are. How awesome, then, to consider that the ultimate seed of our makeup is God—"So God created man in God's own image . . . male and female God created them" reads the biblical account of our origin.

Take time to reflect on your divine heritage.

BIBLE READINGS

Genesis 1:27-31   *Romans 8:12-17*

Day Six

In *The Cloister Walk,* Kathleen Norris tells the story of a woman who grows from an ill-considered infatuation for a celibate priest to a loving, lasting friendship with the man. "My infatuation hadn't taken the real person into account," she eventually explained to Norris. "I found that love starts when you see the real person, not the one you've invented."

We often carry infatuation into our search for God. We imagine a god whom we can understand, a "Daddy Warbucks" who is waiting to give us everything we ask for, a kindly grandparent who asks nothing of us in return. Love for God starts, as does love for another person, when we see past the god we imagine to the reality of the eternal Creator and Sustainer of all life.

In your time with God today, examine what god-qualities may be more invention than reality.

BIBLE READINGS

Deuteronomy 10:12-20   *Mark 12:28-34*

Day Seven

How do I love thee? Let me count the ways." So wrote the poet Elizabeth Barrett Browning to her dearest love, and her evocative lines have survived her now by nearly 140 years. She spoke of a love of multiple facets, and she suggested by it that she had given herself the assignment of thinking about the person she loved with specific, concentrated appreciation.

We sometimes allow our love for God to be an ephemeral, general emotion. But if we give our full attention to who God is and what God has revealed to us, we will enrich our experience and expression. We will be able to "count the ways," and we will find the number of ways will grow and keep on growing.

Reflect now on what you know of God. Let your heart speak to God about it.

BIBLE READINGS

Song of Songs 1:2-4   1 John 4:19-21

I praise you because I am fearfully
    and wonderfully made;
        your works are wonderful,
        I know that full well.
My frame was not hidden from you
        when I was made
        in the secret place.
When I was woven together
        in the depths of the earth,
        your eyes saw my unformed body.
All the days ordained for me
        were written in your book
        before one of them came to be.

How precious to me
        are your thoughts, O God!
        How vast is the sum of them!
Were I to count them,
        they would outnumber
        the grains of sand.

Psalm 139:14–18

CHAPTER THREE

Are You There, God?

ROAD MAPS *and* SIGNPOSTS

SOME YEARS AGO, AFTER ATTENDING A LITERATURE CONFERENCE IN MANKATO, MINNESOTA, I DECIDED IT WAS TIME I SAW THE ROCKY MOUNTAINS. SO I RENTED A CAR AND SET OUT ALONE ACROSS THE PRAIRIES, HEAD-ING WEST WITH ONLY MY ROAD ATLAS AND A DESIRE TO MEET THE ROCKIES FACE-TO-FACE. WELL, THAT'S NOT QUITE TRUE. I ALSO CARRIED WITH ME SOMEWHAT VAGUE MEMORIES OF THINGS I'D LEARNED ABOUT THE ROCKIES when I studied geography in grade school. And I'd seen photographs and paintings of them, as well as at least one motion picture that had the Rockies as its setting. One of my high school friends, who grew up in Wyoming, had described the great range of mountains with such passion and detail that I could almost imagine I knew what it would be like to scale its heights. Of course, I also had detailed information about this geological wonder and advice from those who had been there about what to look for and what to expect.

Nevertheless, I could *only* imagine, and my imagination was necessarily limited by a lack of personal experience. The maps and directions, descriptions and advice, of the experienced became invaluable signposts to making my way to the mountains.

That trip to the Rockies reminds me of our search for God. In the spiritual realm, too, we can have a sense of destination and a desire to reach it, and we need a collection of signposts and signals to guide us on our way. As with the road trip, the navigational aids serve more than one function. They help us to keep our attention focused on the goal of the journey, which is to connect meaningfully with God. They increase our knowledge and understanding of where we are going— that is, they teach us about the God we seek, about ourselves, and about the road between God and us. There, too, we benefit from directions and expert advice to keep us on track and encourage us to continue when we might otherwise give up.

If a physical journey requires focus and knowledge, understanding and courage, how much more does the journey toward God. Because God is Spirit, after all, we do not as readily find our way. We have spiritual equivalents of eyes and ears, hands and feet, but we do not learn to use them as automatically as the physical. And because God is Other—not the same as we are—we seem to need even more guidance than we do in our human connections. The end point of our spiritual journey precedes and exceeds all our ordinary limits.

So, what are the road maps and signposts of the spiritual journey toward God? They are a great variety of messages from God— some in nature, others in human language, still others in human experience—that reveal God, our own natures, the meaning of our lives, and the potential of a personal relationship with the Revealer. The universe itself, *nature* and its mysterious operation, is the first great pointer to God. Add to that *Scripture*, a collection of written works that has stood the test of time as inspired (God-directed) literature unfolding a divine perspective. Our search is guided as well by the creative outpouring of *human giftedness* as it reaches toward and is steered by God. We see God, too, in our *pleasures*, those facets of our lives that enliven and enrich us. Perhaps most mysteriously, we are directed by our *suffering*. All of these show us the way to move closer to God.

I traveled to the Rockies with directions and expectations. I imagined what my destination would look like, how it would feel, and what it would require of me. But nothing anyone could tell me, no second-hand photographic or artistic depiction, no amount of scientific knowledge, could ultimately prepare me for the experience of those awesome masses of Earth's crust, thrusting skyward to the breathless heights. How thrilling as we make our spiritual journey to consider that our most glorious imaginings about God cannot possibly match what awaits us.

Road Maps & Signposts

ANY GOOD TEACHER KNOWS THAT IT TAKES A variety of approaches to reach the broadest possible range of students. Different students perceive in different ways, and not everyone can decipher the same messages to discover meaning. Although one student might best understand sound, for example, by reading about it, another student wouldn't "get it" until she saw a diagram of sound waves. Still another might need a demonstration of how long it takes to hear a noise that occurs a certain distance away. And yet another would learn best by developing experiments for himself. And so on.

As the Master Teacher of all of creation, God has designed messages that speak to our diversity. There's something for everyone who seeks to make the journey Godward. It's natural that some of us are more, or less, drawn to certain styles of revelation and direction from God. And sometimes we may become so enthusiastic about one style or another that we come to believe that we've found *the* revelation of God. Before we consider a number of spiritual road maps and signposts, I want to make a strong plea for balance.

Finding God's Revelation

IN NATURE

IN SCRIPTURE

IN HUMAN GIFTEDNESS

IN OUR PLEASURES

IN OUR SUFFERING

First of all, we can relish the many means by which the Almighty may choose to work in the lives of other people, even when we don't altogether understand or identify with those means. It is in the very diversity of our human race, in how we see, learn, and make connections, that we are most enriched and encouraged.

Second, and just as important, we can embrace a variety of pointers ourselves, expanding our own limits by not focusing on one avenue of God's revelation to the exclusion of others. As we look for God's signposts in more places of our lives, we increase our potential for a vibrant relationship with the One we seek, a relationship that permeates the whole of our life.

So throw open the windows of possibility. We can do no better than to bring an elastic and adventurous spirit to a search that is meant to stretch and shape us. And we can expect that the more open we become to God's messages, the truer our path will become.

GOD'S REVELATION IN NATURE

The Psalmist writes, "The heavens declare the glory of God; the skies proclaim the work of God's hands." I know something about the glassblower by examining the finespun glass sculpture he creates; about the chef by tasting her concoctions; about the teacher by relating to his students. Just so, I know something about the ultimate Creator by experiencing creation. What was made becomes the announcement of the Maker, "declaring" and "proclaiming" qualities that might otherwise remain unknown. We are delighted by the extraordinary beauty, balance, humor, and diversity we see in nature. We are challenged by its complicated systems and interdependencies. We are humbled by nature's power and subject to its forces. We are awed by patterns on a microscopic level that we see repeated throughout nature, even on the cosmic scale. And we are comforted by the obvious attention to detail, the fabulous provision for thousands of living organisms

Tuning in to Nature

PLANT YOURSELF
IN THE MIDST
OF NATURE

BECOME A NATURE
RESEARCHER

ENGAGE IN
FORMAL STUDY

in each and every natural system. All this comes from the One who loves us and welcomes our seeking.

Most wonderful of all, nature is available to everyone in one way or another—even in the heart of a dense city. We do ourselves a disservice when we take the natural world for granted, either by insulating ourselves from it with all our contraptions and climate-controlled spaces or by failing to *notice* nature when it's right in front of us. But simply recognizing that we've turned away from one of God's great instructors can become the first step toward greater conscious-ness. Most especially, if we learn to make nature a regular focus of our attention in the context of time alone with God, we open our eyes and ears to a marvel-filled tutorial.

Perhaps the most direct way to tune in to nature as God's proclamation is to plant ourselves in the midst of nature, to observe it in all its beauty and complexity firsthand.

Plan a regular walk in a forest, a swim in the ocean, some grubbing in the garden, or bird-watching expeditions. Make a point of noticing details all around you. I've found that sitting completely still on a huge rock in the middle of a salt marsh, I've managed often to become "invis-ible" to the wildlife around me. Tiny fiddler crabs come out of hiding, egrets and gulls land to fish just feet away, dragonflies and skimmers resume their extraordinary ordinary lives, all serenaded by the wind whispering through the grasses. I think of it as theater in the rough. Active attention to nature can yield amazing insights and patterns.

Of course, we can make ourselves actual students of nature as well.

Even as simple an exercise as reading some of the exceptional articles that appear in a wide variety of quality nature and environmental magazines can provide an awe-inspiring inside view of nature. Libraries and bookstores abound in beautiful photographic books that detail the wonders of nature around the world and beyond. So, too, do the many documentaries offered by television, home video, and in-the-round movie theaters. Planetariums and natural history museums provide alternative visions of the world we inhabit.

I'd even recommend formal study: college and adult-education courses that many schools offer in human biology, zoology, astronomy, geology, botany, and horticulture.

Vacations and field trips are available as well that focus specifically on some fascinating aspect of the natural world, with expert guides who give a richer, fuller understanding of what you see and experience.

In any or all of these natural encounters, we can find God's signposts if we sincerely seek them and then let God speak to us through them. A student once told me of a difficult, lonely time she had spent in a city far from her country upbringing. "I was so homesick," she said. "I didn't know anyone. And I ached for the sight of something natural." She made it through her first winter in a tiny apartment, filling it with whatever houseplants could survive the meager light filtering through two small windows. Then one spring morning, she awoke to noisy chirping. She discovered that a little swallow had built her nest behind a rain gutter on the window ledge right outside. For weeks the woman watched and waited with the bird for the advent of the chicks. After they had hatched, she observed daily feedings and thrilled to the growth and feathering of the little creatures. Finally, she saw the last of them get its successful flying lesson. "I was heartbroken when they all left," she said. "But then the most miraculous thing happened. Out of the abandoned nest grew a morning glory. Its seed must have been in something the bird fed to her young. I watered the vine and trained it to grow around my window, and all summer I looked through a blooming bower. I knew then that I wasn't alone at all. I was being cared for."

In nature, we feel the Master's touch ourselves.

GOD'S REVELATION IN SCRIPTURE

The Bible—for the Jew the Tanakh, for the Christian the Old and New Testaments—has been translated from its original Hebrew, Aramaic, and Greek into virtually every written language that exists today.

Jews and Christians hold the Bible to be unique in the history of literature, a collection of writings singularly directed by God to reveal the sacred story of God in space and time. It includes history, poetry, songs, and philosophical and prophetic writings, and it conveys eye-witness accounts of people in the presence of the Divine. Its description as the "greatest book ever written" is perfectly accurate. In fact, the Bible stands as the worldwide best-seller of all time.

The study of Scripture has preoccupied people seeking God for as long as it has existed. Unlike the signposts of nature, the Bible offers a road map for action, a moral yardstick against which to measure our lives, and a collection of personal histories that illuminates God's interactions with us.

❧ *You may want to read and study the Bible as an academic discipline.* Many people of faith have found such a practice to be invaluable. A large and ever-increasing number of works have been published to help people read the Bible. All of these have the explicit goal of making the Bible more discernible to those who are not Bible scholars. The study of the Bible, like the study of nature, illuminates the character and qualities of God.

❧ *In contrast to academic Bible study is a quiet reading of some portion of Scripture,* however small, that we then make the focus of reflection for some part of our time alone with God. With this approach to a sacred text, we give the words a chance to sink in, to strike us in a fresh way, or to bring new meaning to insights we've had in the past. We mull over the words and explore their ramifications for our own lives without overlaying them too heavily with the thoughts and interpretations of other people. In this way, too, we make a silent space into which God can speak truth directly. We know that this has happened in the moment that a passage of Scripture we've read a hundred times suddenly seems to jump off the page at us, addressing us as though it were just written and for us alone. David, a student, told me that he had turned to the Psalms during a time when his career seemed to be failing and his wife had just given birth to their third child. "I felt as though I was drowning," he told me. "I've never felt such despair." Then one day he stumbled on Psalm 27. "For in the day of trouble God will keep me safe in his dwelling," David read. "He will hide me in the shelter of his tabernacle and set me high upon a rock." David had read that Psalm many times, but this time he heard in it a promise from God. It gave him the courage to pray, to face his work problems, and to ask for help to keep his family's resources in good order.

Using Scripture to Seek God

APPROACH THE BIBLE AS AN ACADEMIC DISCIPLINE

READ THE BIBLE AND REFLECT IN PRAYER

In Scripture, as in other literature, individuals find some literary styles and content more immediately interesting or arresting than others. I believe that's why God directed a work of such diversity and with so many separate human authors: so that despite our different personalities and personal histories, we would all find a point of identification, a place to begin. It's important to remember, though, that one portion of Scripture often illuminates or interprets another, and to take any of it in complete isolation can lead us to conclusions that may be quite contrary to the real meaning. As we learn more about the background and authorship of the Bible, we develop our ability to reflect on all portions of it with more comprehension.

In our lives and in our time with God, Scripture becomes our interpreter and teacher, drawing us closer to God as we see God more clearly.

GOD'S REVELATION IN HUMAN GIFTEDNESS

We often look outside of ourselves to see God's pointers. But if we believe that we bear in us the divine image, however distorted or disguised, then we can also look within at what we are. Certainly our physical bodies bear the stamp of a grand design; and our mental and emotional capacities—including an innate sense of right and wrong—hint strongly at aspects of the Creator. But perhaps as much or more revealing is what we *do* with what we are.

In *Walking on Water*, Madeleine L'Engle writes: "My faith in a loving Creator of the galaxies, so loving that the very hairs of my head are counted, is stronger in my work than in my life, and often it is the work that pulls me back from the precipice of faithlessness."

Each of us has "work" in this life. By this I mean that each one of us has been gifted by God in a particular way. L'Engle clearly refers to her professional work of writing and public speaking, but I believe that our God-revealing work may or may not be closely related to how we earn a living. It may or may not have the glamour of a great talent in the arts, in science, in sports, or in scholarship. It may or may not earn us appreciation or recognition, money or power, in human affairs. We discover the nature of our giftedness in what we enjoy and can learn to do well.

I am always sorry when I hear another human being assess himself or herself with such a statement as "There's nothing I'm good at. I'll never excel at anything I try to do." It pains me for the sake of that individual because such a low judgment of oneself is in direct conflict with the belief that we bear the image of our Creator, and, for that reason, it causes conflict and sorrow in the one who says it. It hurts me, too, because we humans are related in a mighty web of connectedness. We need each other. Every one of us has the potential to make a meaningful contribution. Not one of us is a throwaway. But modern society has taught us to value some gifts so far above others that we often fail to value in ourselves and others what is uniquely ours or theirs. Every time an individual is diminished by such disregard, we are all diminished. And we impoverish our understanding of the One who is the source of our gifts.

Our giftedness may lie in one of the arenas esteemed by our culture; or it may reside in the way we relate to others, our willingness to do a repetitive job efficiently, our ability to bring humor to any situation, our generosity, our common sense, our dreaminess, our grasp of the way things work, or our spiritual sensitivity. Human beings are almost always a complicated blend of numerous gifts. If and as we come to appreciate more and more the giftedness that exists in ourselves and those around us, we have a clearer, wider view of God available to us.

I think of Stanley, a retired man living in a nearby condominium complex. I see him often walking his dogs on the long dirt lanes that run through the woods in our community. Stanley is a shy, quiet man, but when he thinks he's alone, I've heard him whistle a tune that could make you cry, it's so lovely. His repertoire is eclectic, and he can bring the most amazing expression to each song he offers, as though he were painting with colors and brushstrokes. One day, Stanley and I passed on the path and exchanged our usual few words. "Do you know," he blurted suddenly. "A young woman stopped me back there this morning." He pointed in the direction from which he'd come. She told him she lived in a house nestled deep in the trees and that she could hear him whistling every morning. She went on to explain that her mother had lived with her until she had suddenly died just two weeks before. "My mother was blind," the woman told Stanley, "but she told me before she died that God had been sending her beautiful visions ever since she came to live with me. God sent them to her, she said, on the notes of an angel's whistle."

As far as I know, Stanley is just as much flesh and blood as I am, but in exercising a simple gift with his whole heart, he became an angel, God's messenger, who blessed the final days in this life of a woman who would never see another blue sky or sparkling sea.

For some of us, finding and using our gifts requires courage. Chuck Jones, creator and animator of the much-loved Bugs Bunny and Wile E. Coyote, reflects in *The Creative Spirit*, "Fear is a vital factor in any creative work. The fishermen from the Aran Islands off Ireland, one of the most difficult fishing grounds in the world, say that anybody who doesn't fear the ocean should not go fishing."

It's understandable, even natural, to "fear the ocean" when we consider how we will put our giftedness to work. But if fear is natural and in fact can vitalize our acting out of our gifts, we can face the fear, step beyond it, and come closer to the Originator of our work. We can open the way to become God's angels in this world.

And every time we give our heartfelt and appreciative attention to the giftedness of others, without envy or jealousy, we can know something more about the character and caring of God. We can carry that closeness and knowledge with us into our time alone with God. In that priceless time we can reflect on the closeness and allow our new knowledge to blossom in our soul. ▸

The more we exercise our gifts, the more we experience God's creative work in us and through us, because, in fact, the exercise of our gifts—no matter what form they take—is intrinsically a creative act. It is one way in which we enact the image of God in us. And it is one way that we gain a clearer view of God in one another.

GOD'S REVELATION IN OUR PLEASURES

Wait a minute! God in our pleasures? Aren't pleasures the naughty little somethings that we try to hide from God? There's a strong strain of this idea in modern thinking. We seem to have the idea that all of life is divided into the sacred and the secular—with pleasure firmly planted in the latter—and that the two don't mix. But that is not the message of creation, nor is it the thrust of Scripture. In fact, the survival of our planet depends to some extent on the pleasure we and other species of creatures derive from such fundamental activities as eating, playing, mating, and caring for our young. And Scripture makes very plain that God intends that we be both pleased and grateful for life and all the good in it—not only that, but that we see God's hand in it. "This is the day that the Lord has made," says the Psalmist. "Let us rejoice and be glad in it." The Psalmist doesn't say, "Let us rejoice and be glad in the *religious part* of it," because there is no aspect of life that does not have the potential of the sacred in it. Our ability to feel pleasure at all is as much God's gift as the sun and the rain and the atmosphere that sustain life.

Pleasure arrives in a thousand different packages, attached to a job well done, a game well played, a beautiful place, an intimate connection, a delicious flavor or aroma, or a dramatic sunset. The list is endless.

If our pleasures are to guide us toward God, however, we have to learn to see God in them. A wise and faithful minister once suggested to his congregation that they try a simple exercise. It was a time of the year when the sparrows swooped around and overhead in large, graceful flocks. "Every time you see those birds do their dance," the minister said, "remember their Maker and say, 'Thank you.'" Such a modest amount of consciousness, put into practice, transformed our vision many times every day.

I've thought about that experience often since, and I've reflected on why it had such power. I realize now that seeing the Giver behind the gift of one simple pleasure flowed over into others, and the growing habit made all of life a potential meeting place with God. The physical sensation that accompanies pleasure became a reminder of God's presence and loving provision. Now, in the midst of rousing laughter or spirited play, a beautiful symphony or a scrumptious meal, there is a dimension of sacred attention and thanksgiving. And time alone with God resonates with gratitude for all that pleases in life.

GOD'S REVELATION IN OUR SUFFERING

C.S. Lewis once said, "God whispers to us in our pleasures. God shouts to us in our pain." With each joy and happy surprise, God's whisper says, "I love you this much." With every sorrow, every ache, every loss, God's shout says, "You need me this much." Our pleasures are the buoyant resting places of our lives that energize and elevate us. Our pains are the training ground, the wake-up call, for the kind of gutsy understanding, wisdom, and commitment that turn us firmly toward God.

Letting Suffering Reveal God

REMEMBER OUR
DEPENDENCE

EXPECT GOD'S
ANSWER

ACKNOWLEDGE
GOD'S VIEWPOINT

OPEN OURSELVES
TO LEARN

APPLY WHAT
WE'RE LEARNING

Can I explain why God allows suffering in the world? No, but I can see many ways in which suffering has the potential to make us stronger, more compassionate, more aware of our dependence. And I know that when people seek God in the midst of suffering, looking for understanding in all of God's messages in nature and Scripture, their gifts and their pleasures, they often find hope and courage and a sense of purpose that has otherwise eluded them.

As with God's other road maps, our response to suffering plays the greatest role in how effectively God is revealed in it. We naturally first turn to God in the midst of pain with the request that the Almighty make it go away. There's nothing wrong with such a request; in fact, nothing could be more right, because God is certainly the One who can remove any sorrow. The Bible records a long parade of faithful people who responded to suffering in exactly that way. But here's the challenging truth: At some times, God's answer was, "Okay, I will"; at others, "Not yet"; and at still others, "Not in this lifetime." And the individuals' response at *that* point made all the difference in their lives and in their journey toward God. Those who rejected God's answer grew bitter or despondent, and they neither learned nor grew. Those who accepted God's reply were enabled to wait expectantly for God's alternative.

Consider five phases of seeking God in the face of hardship:

First, we let it remind us of our dependence on our Creator and Sustainer. We ask God for help, for relief, for the end of suffering.

Second, we listen with the expectation that God will answer. This means being prepared that the answer may not be the one for which we hope.

Third, we acknowledge God's divine perspective in the apparent answer we receive. We continue to depend on the One who can and may remove our pain.

At the same time, we open ourselves to what God can teach us in any case.

Finally, we take the truths we learn and put them to work in ourselves and our lives.

Few people welcome suffering—most of us go to great lengths to avoid it. But we will all have our share before we die. Insofar as we let it turn us toward God, let God speak to us through it, and exercise the spiritual muscles that God is inviting us to develop, our suffering can become a powerful engine for good in this life.

Nature. Scripture. Giftedness. Pleasure. Suffering. All God's road maps and signposts offer guidance and revelation. All are gifts from the Creator for the ultimate welfare of our spirits. It's possible, of course, to so immerse ourselves in any one of them that it becomes an end in itself rather than a marker that leads us to God. In the most extreme case, one or another can become a surrogate god, with the result that we worship not God but nature, the Bible, our gifts, pleasure, or even our suffering. But if, instead, we allow all of these to be the servants of our search, we have markers for the greatest journey we will ever make.

Meditations

ON GOD'S ROAD MAPS

The following meditations and Bible readings focus on the map God draws to bring us closer. As you enter another week's commitment to time with God, make sure that your chosen time and place are working for you. If not, make the adjustments that can help you to continue. You may find it encouraging to write down some of your thoughts and prayers. Keep whatever you write so you can come back to it later, when you may be surprised at the insights you have recorded and how meaningful they have become—they may even serve as additional signposts that God uses to direct you.

Day One

A national newspaper recently published what it termed a new "map of the brain." Scientists believe they have found channels, electrical impulses, and chemicals to account for nearly all of human experience, including love, war, and religion.

We can explore and speculate and draw maps of what exists. We can test our theories and "prove" recurring phenomena. We can even "copy" living things through cloning. What we cannot do is to bring the thing we explore, study, map, or copy into existence from nothing. Only God can do that.

What marvel in creation can you explore today in the context of the One who brought it about?

BIBLE READINGS

Isaiah 40:25-26   *Matthew 6:25-34*

Day Two

One of my favorite cartoons shows a man standing at the counter of a bookstore while a salesperson stares at the screen of a computer, hands on the keyboard. "The Bible," the salesperson says. "That would be under self-help."

Self-help—yes. With a profound twist. The Bible writers say that God "breathed" the Scriptures to draw us to a life forever connected to the Life-giver. Such language recalls the description in Genesis of God breathing life into a handful of earth to create humankind.

God's breath made the difference between the dust of the ground and a living being; between a self-help manual and a road map to Life. What part of your life today needs God's life-giving breath?

BIBLE READINGS

Genesis 2:4-7   2 Timothy 3:14-17

Day Three

The theologian Charles Haddon Spurgeon once wrote: "No text has spent itself upon the person who first received it. God's comforts are like wells, which no one person or set of people can drain dry, however mighty may be their thirst."

We may come to the Bible with an idea of what we will find. We may come with what we *want* to find. In both cases, it's like taking a thermos to a mountain spring with orders to "fill'er up." We will never reach the bottom of what God has to say in Scripture. No matter how many have preceded us, and regardless of what they or we have drawn out of Scripture, there remains as much and more still available to us.

Examine your spirit today. Are you parched in some part of your life? Reflect on Scripture with that in mind.

BIBLE READINGS

Isaiah 55:1-3   John 4:7-14

Day Four

*I*n the world of bees, "scouts" fly out to find sources of food, making their way to forests and meadows, our yards, gardens, and orchards, and our picnic tables. The scouts remember the route they took, and they describe it when they return to the hive—create a road map, as it were—by performing a complicated "dance" for the bees in their community that will harvest.

They do what God designed them to do, and their entire hive flourishes. What's more, their work graces human lives with beautiful flowers, enriches our diet with fruits and vegetables, and sweetens our experience with honey.

Consider today in the presence of your Creator what part you may play in the life of the human community.

BIBLE READINGS

Psalm 1   1 Corinthians 12:4-11

Day Five

Reading the first few pages of his new work to a circle of friends, the writer seemed edgy, uncertain, until he began to read. Then the beauty of the prose and the unfolding life of the characters in it took possession of him and his audience. When he stopped reading, a long moment of silence ensued. Then his listeners burst into praise, full of the joy they saw reflected on his face. He suddenly threw his head back, shouted, "Slam dunk!" at the top of his voice, and burst into pure, outrageous laughter.

What better gift exists in life than a moment of consuming joy? How can you carry it with you into your time alone with God?

BIBLE READINGS

1 Chronicles 16:7-13   *Philippians 4:4-9*

Day Six

fter a storm, a rainbow stretches across the heavens to assure us of the sun's return.

After winter, nature comes out of its dormancy and bursts into living color and fertility.

After a forest fire, the earth receives its own back as fertilizer for new and healthy growth.

After labor, a child graces our lives.

We sorrow. God comforts and provides.

BIBLE READINGS

Psalm 23   Matthew 11:28-30

Day Seven

*I*n my older daughter's 13th year, we took a trip together to the coast of Maine. One morning, as we sat on the rocky cliff to watch the sun rise over the water, my daughter suddenly pointed to the rocks below us.

"Those are like us," she said, "and the ocean is like God."

The rocks, she explained, once had jagged edges and rough, cutting surfaces. But over time, the ocean waves and tides, washing again and again over the rocks, smoothed and polished them and exposed their rainbow of colors and patterns.

God intends to bring out the best in us. What polishing is God at work on in you today?

BIBLE READINGS

Proverbs 3:11-12   *Hebrews 12:7-13*

O Lord, our Lord
how majestic is your name
in all the earth!

You have set your glory
above the heavens.
From the lips of children and infants
you have ordained praise
because of your enemies,
to silence the foe and the avenger.

When I consider your heavens,
the work of your fingers,
the moon and the stars,
which you have set in place,
what is man that you are mindful of him,
the son of man that you care for him?
You made him a little lower
than the heavenly beings
and crowned him with glory and honor.

Psalm 8:1–5

CHAPTER FOUR

The
Practice of Seeking

ELEMENTS *of* DISCIPLINE

I N A FRIENDLY DISCUSSION ONE NEW YEAR'S EVE, A MAN I KNOW DECLARED THAT HE HAD STEADFASTLY SWORN OFF NEW YEAR'S RESOLUTIONS. WHY? WE ASKED. DON'T THEY HELP US TO REFLECT ON WHAT WE'VE DONE? DON'T THEY SPUR US TO POSITIVE CHANGE? NOT AT ALL, HE CLAIMED. RESOLUTIONS JUST REMIND US OF OUR PAST FAILURES AND DOOM US TO NEW ONES. I WAS STRUCK IN THE SILENT MOMENT THAT FOLLOWED HIS STATEMENT by the expressions I saw on the faces of his audience. Self-doubt. Fear. Sadness. Resignation. He had touched a chord in each of us, albeit lightly and perhaps unwittingly. The group launched into a good-natured dispute after that, but the first, uneasy pause remained with me.

Since then, I've considered the depth of honest feeling that man conveyed. He was right that many a resolution falls by the wayside in the days, weeks, or months after we've promised ourselves a particular course of action. Perhaps that's why it takes such an act of courage to begin any practice that holds the potential to transform our life. We are assaulted by past disappointments, and we doubt our ability to choose differently in the future. In fact, all sorts of circumstances, behavior patterns, and attitudes can complicate our best intentions. The initial courageous decision to begin requires discipline—an ongoing process of our will—to continue a course day after day.

We have to regularly exercise our bodies and minds, for example, to become skilled and learned, and the more serious we are about any area of growth, the more self-discipline we need in the strengthening practices that will take us forward. Every successful athlete goes through the basic calisthenics, drills, practices, and study needed to produce a top performance. So, too, the artist, the scholar, the artisan, and the engineer. Our spiritual life requires no less, and we find our training in the daily habits that connect us to God, not only as individuals but in the community as well.

Theologian Richard J. Foster calls discipline "the path to spiritual growth." We put ourselves on the path in pursuit of a life firmly and daily connected to the sacred, a life that can thereby grow and transform our character, our ideas, our way of relating to God and others. The path itself does not produce the changes in us. It places us where change can occur—that is, in the presence and power of the One who can change us. Our responsibility lies in getting on the path and staying there. God does the rest.

So how do we not only resolve to find time alone with God but make it a lifelong discipline? One way, certainly, involves identifying our personal pitfalls and learning how to deal with them directly. But before we do that, we need to take a look at the positive elements of discipline that bolster our intentions and carry us forward.

Elements of Discipline

IN THE NATIONAL DRIVE TO EDUCATE AMERICAN youth on the dangers of drug use and abuse, the catchphrase "Just say no" entered our popular lexicon. It appeared on billboards and

T-shirts, in pamphlets and TV ads. It conveyed the underlying message that it is in the individual's power to choose, to say yes or to say no to all the wild variety of possibilities (in this case, including drugs) that present themselves to us daily. Many people—usually adults and many, I suspect, feeling defeated in some area of their own lives—met that campaign with more than a touch of cynicism. "Yeah, right," they said. "If it were that easy, we wouldn't have the problems we do with addiction, overeating, overspending, and so on."

I believe that the people promoting "Just say no" were on the right track toward the only solution to social and personal challenges. Unless we recognize and accept responsibility for our own life and choices, we cannot hope to shape the life we want. But I sympathize with the naysayers as well. We do not automatically find within ourselves the ability to "Just say no" or "Just do it" or "Deal with it" when the time comes to exercise our discipline muscles. We have to grow into that capability.

Underlying any discipline are common elements that allow us to learn and develop its practice. The first—*orientation*—relates to making what we hope for in the long run work for us in the short run. The second—*observation*—has to do with using the whole of our life and experience to fuel our intention. The third—*concentration*—refers to developing the skills needed to focus the prac-

Elements

ORIENTATION

OBSERVATION

CONCENTRATION

APPLICATION

HEART OF
DISCIPLINE

tice of our discipline. The fourth—*application*—deals with what we take from the discipline to continue to build. All of these elements play an important role in the discipline of time with God.

THE FIRST ELEMENT *Orientation*

I had my first powerful lesson in the importance of orientation when three other women and I chartered a sailboat for a 10-day journey along the eastern seaboard. Among us, only one was an experienced sailor. The rest of us became her students under sail.

I had often watched with longing the graceful, silent glide of the sailing vessels I could see from the shore. And somehow I had the impression that sailing the sea was much like driving a highway. You just followed the signs. It wasn't until I was out on the open water that I realized how very different navigation on water could be. Landmarks become less obvious when they are located miles away. Dangers and challenges, such as tides and currents, shallows and jagged rocks, often lie hidden under the constant rolling surface of the sea. Distances are impossible to discern by sight over the endless expanse of water. And there is no pulling off at the next rest stop to ask directions.

So we familiarized ourselves with the language of the navigation charts. We came to recognize the markings for water depth, landmark height, and underwater hazards. We learned to translate symbols for navigational aids, both land-bound and floating. Most important, we practiced under the tutelage of our skipper the rudiments of charting a course and following it. When sailing, I discovered, it is not sufficient to know where you started, where you are, and where you're heading. You need another location—a reliable fixed point of reference by which to chart your course and stay on it. Throughout your journey, you orient yourself by fixed points, checking your progress and direction against them, turning back to them again and again.

Making God Our Orientation

TAKE PART IN RELIGIOUS OBSERVANCES

CREATE PERSONAL REMINDERS OF GOD

REMEMBER THAT THE JOURNEY HAS AN END

Our lives in this present existence have a beginning point and an end point. But the distance we travel between those two points can seem as mysterious and confusing as a great ocean. The time we spend with God provides the opportunity to chart a true course, if we make God our fixed point of reference. And when we keep our reference point in mind throughout the remaining hours and minutes of our days, we grow in our desire to seek God's presence—to return, as it were, to the navigational chart that keeps us on course.

How do we make God our orientation?

❧ *Certainly we can participate in community reminders of God's presence*—whether in weekly worship services, baptisms, bar mitzvahs and bas mitzvahs, holy days, confirmations, daily masses, or religious weddings. Often, when describing commemorations and ceremonies, Bible writers included God's injunction to "do this in remembrance of Me." Religious rituals and observances are God's gift to us for the express purpose of helping us make God our orientation. We accept the gift by participating mindfully, fixing our attention on the spiritual signif-icance of the event, reflecting on what it tells us about God and humankind, and looking for what it can reveal in our own lives.

Further, we can create our own regular reminders to focus on God. We may find certain natural objects that evoke a sense of God's presence and provision. We may discover works of literature or art that bring some aspect of God's character powerfully to mind. We may come to cherish certain passages of Scripture or pieces of music for the spir-itual significance they have for us. A friend of mine found a gorgeous, unblemished nautilus shell on a trip that turned into a time of intense spiritual seeking. That shell has become a centerpiece on the small corner table where this person meets God daily. I have hung an illu-minated, framed passage from a poem by John Donne on my study wall that powerfully captures for me an aspect of seeking God. We can incor-porate any of these into the landscape of our daily lives to make our orientation more and more God-directed.

Finally, we can remember that we are on a journey that will have an earthly end point. We have only shadow pictures and intuitions about the nature of existence beyond the death of our bodies, but we can be sure that God is as present there as here. How we live now has meaning and purpose before an eternal God, and we cooperate in the sacred potential for our existence when we live consciously with reference to the One who gave us life.

THE SECOND ELEMENT *Observation*

Researchers have demonstrated that we sense at all times far more than we are aware of noticing. This more thorough, subconscious awareness allows us to react reflexively, to move through spaces without collisions, to pick up the moods and reactions of other people and animals.

The fact that we're picking up so much of the stimuli around us suggests that we are capable of consciously paying attention to far more of it than we typically do. We call it the "power of observation" in people who manage to increase their awareness of what they see, hear, smell, feel, and taste. For certain professionals, greater awareness may spell the difference between mere competence and exceptional performance. What distinguishes the outstanding doctor, for example? What makes one mechanic better at finding and fixing the problem than another? What elevates one artist to extraordinary expressions while another remains forever no more than a good technician in his or her medium? And what gives one historian so much truer a grasp of the patterns and meanings that ripple through the annals of the past and into the present? Talent? Maybe, but even raw talent has its limits. I believe that at the heart of the difference lies the ability and will to observe.

Over time, purposeful observation—what has sometimes been called "mindfulness"—allows us to weave the multiple threads of life into a meaningful, intriguing web of connections. In the spiritual realm, we can disconnect time with God from everyday life to the point that we tend toward what folk language has termed "so heavenly minded, we're no earthly good." And when life throws the next curveball, we fail to see the relevance and help to be pulled from the sacred connection we've begun. To draw on an earlier metaphor, we set our sailing course by that essential fixed point, then proceed to ignore tides, wind direction, currents, the condition of our boat, and all the other boats in the water. The net result, of course, is spiritual naïveté and a frustrating disconnection of our spiritual life from the rest of our existence.

Practicing Observation

SIMPLY OBSERVE FOR FIVE MINUTES

TAKE A CONSCIOUS WALK

IMAGINE YOURSELF IN THE SHOES OF ANOTHER

TRACE THE ORIGINS OF A SINGLE ITEM

As we put observation to work for us in our spiritual life, we build a bridge from our soul to our concrete, everyday existence. In this way, we fuel a spiritual curiosity—a hunger—that inspires us to return to the discipline of time with God. We want to know more. We want to test what we've seen and intuited in the presence of God, to uncover the ramifications and revelations that grow from what we discover.

The ability to observe carefully begins with conscious intent. With practice, our skill at observation can grow until it becomes a habit that serves us throughout our life.

❧ *Try, for example, planting yourself in one place for just five minutes.* Take note of everything around you, especially those things that you ordinarily take for granted. Choose, for example, a room in which you spend of lot of time. Notice all the objects in it. Think about how they relate to each other, where they come from, what they mean to you, and what they mean to others. Consider their relative importance to the life of your spirit. Ask yourself whether you are sufficiently grateful for their existence. Try this with a storage space or your backyard or a favorite spot in your hometown.

❧ *Take a conscious walk.* As you go, put all extraneous thoughts aside. Think only about the sights and sounds and smells around you. Feel how your feet move with each step, pay attention to which muscles you use and how they work together. Feel your breathing and your heartbeat. Notice the movement of air on your skin. Look—*really* look—at everything along the way. Reflect on the One who designed your body and placed you on your particular patch of the universe.

❧ *Stop for coffee alone at a local café and watch what goes on around you.* Observe the interactions of people. Look at how people move, how they interact, what they wear, what their facial expressions and body language convey. Listen to the noise of the place, then practice isolating one source of the noise at a time. Imagine yourself in the shoes of another, so that his or her life takes on an importance for you, if only for a moment, equal to your own. Imagine God's attention directed equally to each and every one.

❦ *Notice a single item and trace its origins in your imagination.* An upholstered chair, for example, required lumber, nails, tacks, springs, and glue for its frame; fibers, looms, dye, and a design for its fabric; batting and stuffing for its cushioning; distribution and shipping for its sale. Behind each of these elements stand raw materials in their natural environment, inventions, and dozens of human lives, all cooperating in some marvelous dance to produce the chair in which you will read your paper, cuddle your child, rest your weary bones, or carry on a significant conversation. Behind the raw materials, technology, and the human lives themselves stands the Creator and Sustainer of it all. Take the time to notice the material aspects of your life and appreciate how they happen to be there.

Observation is a free gift to every one of us. It reveals the intricacies of an existence that teems with relationships and offers unlimited fascination and insight. If we choose, we can let our power of observation expand the canvas of our view of God, adding detail and color, and enlivening our sense of all that we do not yet know.

THE THIRD ELEMENT *Concentration*

In *Care of the Soul,* Thomas Moore writes that "spirituality demands attention, mindfulness, regularity, and devotion. It asks for some small measure of withdrawal from a world set up to ignore soul." What he is getting at is concentration. When we pursue the discipline of regular time with God, we engage in a radical departure from the typical in our modern world. Giving the life of our soul such special attention is, for the most part, off the beaten track. With so many competing demands in our lives, time with God requires an extra measure of mindfulness that I'll call spiritual concentration.

Orientation gives us a reference point in the midst of everyday living. Observation lets us take in all the wonderful detail of life and use it to feed our spiritual life. Concentration is the courageous step out of our routine existence, with all its distractions and demands, that allows us to focus our attention entirely on God. It is an act of intention that enables us to enter a clutter-free zone. The act leads to the freedom to meet God.

Anne described to me how difficult she had found it to keep spending regular time with God. "I wanted to be closer to God," she said, "and I suspected that the only way that would happen was to make God-time a habit." But her time with God felt like drudgery to her, a chore to be gotten through. Invariably, when she entered into the time she had made for God, she would be overcome with a sense of panic and confusion. "I had so many other things waiting for me," she said. "I kept thinking, 'Hurry up and make something happen.'" And, of course, nothing did.

Further conversation revealed that it took a family crisis and a book on relaxation techniques to transform her time with God. "My daughter was diagnosed with cancer," she explained. "Suddenly, I understood what it meant to put everything in its place. Nothing mattered to me but my daughter, her treatment and healing. Anything else could be put on hold for the duration."

The stress of the situation left her sleepless and plagued with headaches. Reluctant to rely on drugs that could sap her energy, she turned to relaxation exercises to deal with both problems.

"I guess it seems like a roundabout way to discover what was wrong with my time with God," she says now. "But faced with the possibility that my daughter's illness could kill her, I knew how much I wanted that connection to God. And I realized that I'd been playing at it before. I was just dropping by on my way to all those other things in my life. I wasn't giving God my best and full attention. I couldn't have heard God's voice if God had used a bullhorn."

To Concentrate

MOVE DISTRACTIONS OUT OF SIGHT

USE OBJECTS TO FOCUS YOUR ATTENTION

CHOOSE ONE PLACE FOR TIME WITH GOD

CHOOSE A SPOT WHERE YOU WON'T BE DISTURBED

PAY ATTENTION TO COMFORT

The very relaxation techniques that helped her to sleep and relieved her headaches helped her to give God her "best and full attention." She learned how to concentrate—to put herself squarely on the path—so that God could meet her there. In the process, she realized the utmost importance of this spiritual meeting.

Concentration relies on a conducive environment. It is enhanced by physical comfort. And it demands a state of mind that is capable of focus. There will always be times when one or all of these facets of concentration are less than ideal, but if we are aware of their helpfulness, we can take steps to work on them.

When choosing your location for time with God, keep concentration in mind. Consider what is most likely to distract you and do your best to eliminate it. Remember that distractions can be subtle. Your attention may be drawn away without you realizing it, until suddenly, you're aware that you've "lost your place." When that happens, retrace your steps to what first diverted you.

If you find it easiest to use a location at home, look for small ways to move reminders of home chores, hobbies, appointments, and routines out of your range of vision.

If a certain object symbolizes your connection with God in some special way, let it serve your intention to focus by placing it nearby. This may be your Bible, a framed poem, a cherished gift related to some religious rite of passage, or even a prayer journal.

❧ *It may be helpful to always use the same place* for your time alone with God. When you do so, the place itself becomes associated primarily with that special time.

❧ *If you choose a location away from home,* make sure that it's one where you feel safe and where you won't be interrupted.

❧ *Pay special attention to your physical comfort.* Sitting in a position, in a place, or on a piece of furniture that makes you uncomfortable is bound to distract you. By the same token, it's best to avoid times and places in which you are so comfy you become drowsy. Ideally, your physical state should not even enter your mind.

Your mental state may be the hardest to position well for time with God. Anne needed to relax and to get her priorities in order to be truly present in her time with God. Numerous relaxation techniques exist that may help you to put aside the preoccupations you carry with you—deep breathing, simple stretches, focusing exercises. In addition, a journal in which you record your thoughts, prayers, and intentions may help you to concentrate on where you are and with Whom. Finally, speaking directly to God—acknowledging in prayer and meditation that you are not alone but, rather, in the presence of Another—can help to put your head and your heart in the same place.

As we learn to concentrate on the presence of God, we make it possible to hear that still, small voice of the Divine that people of faith have cherished for as long as people have existed.

THE FOURTH ELEMENT *Application*

We come to time with God not only, or even primarily, to reach out to God but to be reached. We place ourselves before the Divine because we want to be connected to something better and bigger and more substantial than ourselves. We put ourselves on the path not because we have to be *someplace*, and it looks like as good a place as any, but because we long for transformation and enlightenment and deliverance from ultimate isolation.

At the heart of discipline is a growing understanding of ourselves and our limits. Certain limits we will never in this life exceed—we won't live forever, we won't know everything, we won't be a star in every arena. But other limits are changeable—we can develop skills, build muscles, develop an expertise, master a body of learning. We have spiritual limits as well. Pride, fear, anger, pettiness, the hurts and resentments we cling to, the hatreds and prejudices we struggle against—all of these constitute real limits on the forward motion of our characters and our lives. And they have a spillover effect on virtually every part of life, whether it's relationships, performance, or simple joy, peace, and hope in our own hearts.

Some spiritual boundaries have to do with humanness. We are not now, nor will we ever be God. We are not infinite, all-knowing, all-powerful, or indestructible. We cannot create energy and matter out of nothing. Neither can we take a handful of dust and breathe form and life into it to create another human being, as Scripture describes God doing. Some spiritual limits, however, have more to do with the ways in which God's image in us is distorted by actions or attitudes that fall short of God's perfection. It is these limits that we bring to the search for God in hope of healing and growth.

If we want any discipline to yield its full potential in and through us, we have to learn the lessons it's offering and grow from them. Time with God becomes most meaningful when we learn to ask, "What is God saying to me in this?" "What does God want me to see? to understand?" Most of all, "What does God want me to be?" Then we listen from our heart and use our head. We keep ourselves on the path and give God room to transform us. Over time, we gain a growing legacy of positive change, and it encourages us to go on.

THE FIFTH ELEMENT *Heart of Discipline*

Some time ago, a movie appeared, with the name *The Fifth Element.* The theme of the story centered, as so many do, on the struggle between good and evil, and the story itself was built on the imagery of the four natural elements—earth, wind, water, and fire—plus one. Not until the movie's denouement did the exact nature of that fifth element become clear. The fifth element was love.

It is ultimately not by *willpower* that we continue in the discipline of time with God, and thus experience transformation, but by God's power. A teeth-gritting determination will leave us weary and resentful. A steady, human-size effort to practice the elements of discipline that help us say yes to time with God day after day will open the way to God's ongoing presence and power. And at the heart of God's presence is love—love for each of us both as we are and as we can be. Over time, as we sense and understand more and more of the love God extends toward us, that love can kindle in us an answering devotion. That, more than all the rest, will draw us to seek God.

Meditations

ON DISCIPLINE

You are steadily building a habit as you continue to seek God through prayer and meditation, Bible reading and reflection. As always, take an honest look at the logistics of your meeting time with God and make the adjustments necessary. As you consider the following thoughts and readings on discipline, pay special attention to those things in your life that may be tempting you to be less faithful in coming to God. Include such observations in the record you started to keep as you considered the road maps and signposts God provides. Just taking the opportunity to notice these temptations can be a strong antidote and help you to continue.

Day One

*H*erman Wouk, in *This Is My God*, described his decision as a young man to embrace the life of observant Judaism. "I took the chance," Wouk wrote, "saying to myself, 'I may be wrong.'" If he hadn't taken that leap, he came to believe, faith would have remained a closed book to him. "There are many things that you can come to know," he wrote, "only by trying to do them."

We cannot know the taste of honey until we touch it to our tongue. We cannot know the comfort of a friend's embrace until we allow ourselves to be touched. And we cannot know the face of God until we turn and look in God's direction.

How can you then draw even closer to God? What step can you take today that moves you in the right direction?

BIBLE READINGS

Micah 7:7   *Hebrews 12:2*

Day Two

*I*n her wise book *Necessary Losses,* Judith Viorst reminds us that every human life involves a series of bereavements. We cannot be full adults without leaving our parents. We cannot gain mastery in a given discipline without forgoing some time devoted to other pursuits we greatly enjoy. We cannot honor a monogamous commitment without giving up past and future lovers. And we cannot love other human beings without eventually facing the pain and sorrow of separation or death.

We do not easily give up anything we love or depend on, yet, as Viorst states, without the losses we cannot grow. If we understand the place of loss in our life, we find at every stage of life what Viorst calls "opportunities for creative transformations."

Consider what you may fear to lose as you turn toward God. Then reflect on what you stand to gain.

BIBLE READINGS

Joshua 22:1-5   Luke 16:13-15

Day Three

When Claude Monet painted, he had in mind a specific way of perceiving and capturing reality on canvas. It was not the landscape per se that he longed to depict but, rather, the endlessly varying effects of light on the landscape. He became an observer of something so evanescent that he had to move among half a dozen easels throughout the day, depending on the direction and mood of the light. He also had to put aside preconceptions about what he saw and how to represent it through the medium of paint because he was on an artistic journey of discovery that required an open mind and a receptive spirit.

When we become spiritual observers, we launch the same kind of journey. An observant spiritual life becomes a grand adventure, and we find unexpected connections and surprising new vistas.

Today, observe the scenery and your relationships with an eye to how God's presence may be revealed. How does this view affect your vision of God?

BIBLE READINGS

Psalm 8   Acts 17:22-25

Day Four

The saying goes, "One picture is worth a thousand words."

At the conclusion of the 20th century, with the prevalence of the print media surrounding us at every pass, we have become a wordy bunch. But we have also come to a greater appreciation of the power of a picture. We have learned to think in metaphors—"the rock of Gibraltar," "a box of chocolates," "a candle in the wind"—in which visual images evoke ideas and enhance our understanding of them.

When we let the physical world all around us "speak," we open ourselves to new levels of thought and feeling. And when we let all we experience "speak" in spiritual language—focused on God and in search of God's truth—we open our hearts to the voice of God in a dramatic and enriching way.

Today, make a record of the images that particularly strike you and reflect on them in the presence of God.

BIBLE READINGS

Isaiah 40:6-8   Mark 4:1-20

Day Five

A magnifying glass takes parallel rays of sunlight and concentrates them by refraction at a single point of convergence. Instead of numerous rays that may give some warmth and light, they become a single power beam capable of starting a fire.

Consider how you may bend the various threads of thought and concern in your mind today so that they converge on God. Watch for ways in which your growing concentration affects your time with God.

BIBLE READINGS

Exodus 33:1-11   Luke 5:16

Day Six

Whoever first said that there is no such thing as secondhand faith hit on a profoundly simple reality. If we want to grow a connection with God, we ourselves open a way for it to happen by seeking God's presence. We may find the experience of others inspiring. We may be warmed by the evidence of others' faith. But we do not have the connection ourselves. Dag Hammarskjöld put it another way: "Only your immediate experience . . . can provide the soil in your soul where the beauty of the whole can grow."

When we seek God sincerely, we open ourselves to an immediate experience of the Divine. We make ourselves a plantable part of the field. The lives of many people of faith give ample evidence that as we open ourselves to God, we can wait expectantly for the Divine presence to make us part of "the beauty of the whole."

What direct connections have you had with God? Reflect on the immediate experiences of today as you seek God's presence.

BIBLE READINGS

Exodus 34:29-35   2 Corinthians 3:18

Day Seven

Joan Baez stood before a crowded auditorium recently. She was honoring a special request that she sing her own rendition of "Swing Low, Sweet Chariot." For the number, she dismissed her backup musicians, stepped away from the microphones and amplifiers, and sang out in a clear, true voice that projected to the far back of the last balcony. When she had finished, the audience went wild, and Baez finally raised her hands for quiet. She said, "I can't take credit for the voice. I'm just responsible for maintenance and delivery."

Each of us has a "voice" that is uniquely our own, a gift direct from God. When we come to God with a receptive spirit, we take the first step toward responsible maintenance and delivery. It is the heart of a simpler spirit, waiting and listening for God to show us how.

Reflect on the "voice" God has given you. What step may God be encouraging you to take with it today?

BIBLE READINGS

Psalm 19:12-14   James 1:22

O, how I love your law!
    I meditate on it all day long.
Your commands make me wiser
    than my enemies,
    for they are ever with me.
I have more insight than all my teachers,
    for I meditate on your statutes.
I have more understanding than the elders,
    for I obey your precepts.
I have kept my feet from every evil path
    so that I might obey your word.
I have not departed from your laws,
    for you yourself have taught me.
How sweet are your words to my taste,
    sweeter than honey to my mouth!
I gain understanding from your precepts;
    therefore I hate every wrong path.

Psalm 119:97–104

CHAPTER FIVE

Standing on Holy Ground

ASPECTS *of* INTIMATE WORSHIP

O N THE COAST OF MAINE, IN AN AREA OF DEEP FOREST, STANDS A GROVE OF PINES THAT THE LOCALS HAVE DUBBED "CATHEDRAL WOOD." THE PINES GROW STRAIGHT UP AND FREE OF BRANCHES FOR 50 OR 60 FEET, AND THE NEEDLE-CARPETED GROUND CREATES SUCH A HUSH UNDERFOOT THAT ONLY THE SOUGHING OF WIND IN THE TREETOPS DISTURBS THE SILENCE. RAYS OF SUNLIGHT STRETCH TO REACH THE FOREST FLOOR in what we, as children, used to call "the fingers of God." When I consider worship, my first thought is often of Cathedral Wood.

The word *worship* has a wide variety of associations for people who have been raised with a formal religious affiliation. We most likely think first of the place or places where we have participated in weekly services of some kind. We connect worship as well with the religious service we know best. We think of liturgies, doctrines, certain styles of music or chanting, choirs or cantors, and particular versions of Scripture. For many of us, the idea of worship includes formal teaching from a minister, rabbi, or priest. And almost without exception, it includes community prayer—prayer by or on behalf of the group.

But "worship," in its essence, requires none of this. It is simply sincere reverence, a response that acknowledges the nature and being of God. Worship does not depend on a group of people, although it can occur there. Worship does not need a trained leader or a canon of religious songs or a set form. Rather, worship is an act of the human spirit—a heart-centered answer to the experience of God's presence—that emanates from an individual soul. When I stand in Cathedral Wood and lift my gaze to the filtered rays of sun, transfixed with awe at the One who created it all, I worship. Just as truly as—sometimes more than—when I take part in the activities of a Sabbath service.

The writer of the book of Exodus tells the story of how God captured Moses' attention in the desert one day. Moses saw a bush that, although it was on fire, did not burn up. When he came close to investigate this mystery, God spoke to him from within the bush, warning Moses to come no closer without taking off his shoes. Why? "The place where you are standing," God said, "is holy ground." Holiness is the quality of being entirely separated from the commonplace and imbued with the qualities of the divine. Wherever God is present—whether in a formal place of worship, a cathedral wood, or a human heart—is holy ground. When we honor and show respect for who God by nature is, when we give God due credit, or worth-ship, and recognize our own otherness, we "remove our shoes" in worship.

Aspects of Intimate Worship

WHAT DOES IT LOOK LIKE, IN THE PRIVACY OF our own time with God, to remove our shoes in worship? When I once asked this question of a study group—people who were engaged in the habit of regular time with God—I was amazed at the variety and creativity of the answers they gave. They spoke of standing, sitting, even lying down, in certain postures. They described raising their arms, folding their hands, lifting their faces, bowing their heads; they mentioned speaking, singing, chanting, listening to music, playing musical instruments, painting, writing, dancing, and being absolutely still in meditation.

In essence, as they demonstrated, any activity, thought, or expression we direct reverently toward God can be part of personal worship.

Intimate Worship

SILENCE
SHOUTS
RITUAL ACTIONS

Sometimes our best responses to the presence of God happen in stillness and silence. At other times, our heart demands what amounts to great shouts toward God. At still others, we perform ritual actions that symbolize to us the holy ground of God's presence (perhaps even literally removing our shoes!).

In all cases, we bring our spirit to the enterprise of concentrating with a single focus on the divine.

WORSHIPING IN SILENCE

A swarm of paper wasps is determined to build a wing for themselves off the eave of my house. I've been watching them for several days, and as often as I come around to take a look, I hear the buzz of their activity. If one evening I knock down what they've built so far, I'll find them hard at work the next morning, patching and rebuilding. As long as the day lasts, they keep moving and buzzing, and I've been struck by how much they remind me of the human activity in my busy part of the world.

The pace of technology and the habits of hurry often tempt us to live a swarming life. We install noise in every room of our house, in our cars, and on the job, with televisions, computers, and sound systems. We look for faster ways to get where we're going and do what we're doing so we can pack more business into each 24 hours. We interpret "down" time as an opportunity to make more plans or to join a program for health, culture, or structured play.

Unlike the paper wasps, however, whose entire existence centers on accomplishing the specific task their biological coding demands, we humans have been given the gift of consciousness. We have the ability and the inclination to live sometimes on a plane other than that of activity and buzz. We can think. We can reflect and choose. We can laugh and philosophize and experience irrational emotions. And, believe it or not, we can be still.

When we come to our time with God, it's possible to bring our swarming habits with us and not even know it. Emily, a lifelong friend and mentor of mine, lived the whole of her life in busy service to God —she considered it her mission in life to be "used up" in service. An exceptional educator, she taught, opened her home and family to religious meetings and Bible studies, and shared in the leadership of a school and a succession of churches. In the later years of her long life, she suffered from an accumulating number of ailments, such that she was eventually confined to her apartment and, finally, to a chair. Yet she continued to study Scripture, read, and engage in lively discussion with the many friends and students who came to be in her company.

Then Emily's worst fear was realized. Macular degeneration took her eyesight and, with it, the one avenue still open to her for independent activity of some kind. We all did our best to find ways that she could continue, with books on tape and other aids. But after 80-odd years of reading and study, it was a nearly impossible transition for her to make.

Within the year after her sight had gone, I went to visit Emily and was surprised to find her full of excitement. "I've been wondering why I'm still here," she told me. "I've asked God why I remain in this failing body while my husband and so many of my friends and colleagues have long gone. What's the point of continuing here when I can't *do* anything useful?"

Emily told me she had reached a point of deep depression—almost despair—when she realized what her busy life and her expectations about it had failed to show her. "It's enough simply to *be,* in the presence of God," she said. "Without any props or programs, even without words."

In the final days of her life on Earth, Emily discovered a facet of connectedness to God that we of the space age easily miss: silence. The prophet Habakkuk recorded God's declaration: "The Lord is in his holy temple; let all the earth be silent before him." Why? In that case, people had filled their lives with lesser gods, with things they had made, and with wars and God-less activity. Only if they stopped and entered a state of silence before God would they be able to see past their full but misdirected lives to reconnect to their Creator.

God spoke as well through the words of the Psalmist: "Be still and know that I am God; I will be exalted among the nations, I will be exalted in the earth." Exalting God—giving God worth-ship—requires finally that we cease our constant busyness and babble long enough to "know" the Divine.

To Worship in Silence

SUSPEND CERTAINTY

SUSPEND SELF-CENTEREDNESS

SUSPEND SHOPPING-LIST PRAYERS

It takes something to worship in silence. In this age—perhaps in any age, judging by the ancient texts—we do not come to it naturally or easily. But awareness of the option, even the need, for silence lets us take the first step in that direction. We can continue toward worshipful silence with a conscious decision and a number of changes.

First, we suspend certainty. When we think we already know all we're going to know, we tend to be very poor listeners. When we recognize that we don't know, silence for the sake of learning becomes more compelling. In worship, we wait in silence to know God.

❧ *Second, we suspend self-centeredness.* That internal voice that rules so much of our thought time—"I want, I need, I can, I can't, I am, I do," and so on and so forth—can be turned off. Every time the first person singular enters our mind, we can consciously turn our attention Godward. When we exercise the discipline to do so, we open a silent place into which God can speak.

❧ *Third, we suspend our demands.* Our prayers often consist solely of a shopping list of needs and concerns. But if we are silent, steeping (like tea leaves) in God's presence, we absorb a truer sense of the Almighty. Our needs have a different appearance in the light of the One who knows them better than we, and we come to discover more readily the provisions God is making available to us.

As we focus in silence on the Object of our worship, we get a break from our natural preoccupation with our own concerns, a respite our spirits sorely need. In fact, the closer we come to pure worship, the more likely we are to be struck dumb in sheer awe at the greatness and glory of our life's Master Designer.

WORSHIPING WITH SHOUTS

There is a jubilant traditional song, named for its refrain, that has found its way into today's popular music: "How Can I Keep From Singing?" Without remembering any more of the song than that one line, I imagine someone erupting into an irrepressible expression of affirmation. Some wonderful reality has seized the singer by the vocal cords, and it requires relief in much the same way that happiness must at times be relieved by laughter. The singer is full to the bursting point with a great good emotion.

God's presence sometimes reduces us to awed silence. But it can also, just as wonderfully, move us to exuberance. We discover utterly anew or from a new angle some quality of God's power. We sense at a deeper level God's love and care for us. We experience some special evidence of God's infinite trustworthiness. We fill to overflowing with how marvelous it is, and we cannot keep from shouting.

How do we give voice to God-centered joy and enthusiasm? The Bible refers to shouts of joy, singing, dancing, playing musical instruments, clapping hands, writing or reciting poetry, and offering verbal praise. Shouts of worship have as much potential for variety as the people doing the shouting. Anne carries her flute out to a grassy riverbank and pours her praise into its music. William speaks aloud, reciting as prayers passages from Scripture that describe God's character. Leslie writes out her shouts in a journal. Stan gives a stadium-style cheer in a moment of heartfelt thanksgiving. Our individual temperament and talents, cultural background and natural style, can all combine to give us a unique voice before God. No

To Worship With Shouts

BE HONEST

BE FREE

BE CREATIVE

BE ORIGINAL

BE INTELLIGENT

prescription exists for our solo shouts, as long as our enthusiasm expresses a genuine, reverent response to God.

Whatever the form, worshipful shouts are an essential aspect of our time alone with God. If we seek the greatest potential for a true divine connection, we do well to develop this part of worship. We can start by paying attention to particular qualities of a Godward response.

❧ *To begin, let your shouts be honest.* What do you truly see and respond to in God? That's where you should start when you express yourself in worship. You can be sure that God knows the difference between lip service and real worship. Interestingly, the more we focus on certain divine characteristics and offer praise for them, the more we begin to notice and appreciate other ones.

❧ *Let your shouts be free.* It's worth the trouble and ingenuity to find times and places, at least every now and then, in which you can forget how you look or sound as you worship. Self-consciousness squelches spontaneity and inhibits joy. Many people, including me, regularly look for quiet places in nature where we can be expressive without being overheard. We may also save some of our time with God for moments when we're alone at home. In the presence of God, we have nothing to hide, simply because it's impossible to hide anything from God. Nowhere can we express ourselves so freely, and that free expression releases more of what God intends us to be. It sometimes releases aspects of ourselves we never fully knew before.

✤ *Let your shouts be creative.* If you were to gather flowers and arrange them beautifully, all the while praising their Maker, who is to say that that is not an act of worship. I remember a retired chef who volunteered his time in a soup kitchen in my community. The whole time he worked to prepare wholesome, delicious group meals, he sang at the top of his voice. Both the cooking and the songs were directed toward God in worship. He served those in need out of love for God, and his songs were offerings of praise and thanksgiving.

✤ *Let your shouts also be original.* What others have chosen to shout about, or the way they've chosen to express themselves before God, doesn't have to define our own worship. We may find a piece of music, a poem, a prayer, or a painting that inspires our shout of worship, but we make something completely new of it when we respond with all our being. Further, we may discover some impetus to worship—a grand gallop on the back of a horse, say—that has never occurred to anyone we know. It is no less valid for being unusual or seeming odd to others.

✤ *Finally, let your shouts be intelligent.* Enthusiasm is a gift from God. But it can also be disconnected to who and what God really is. One of the best arguments for including Scripture regularly in our time alone with God is the wealth of information and revelation it provides on the nature and purposes of God in relation to humankind. One of the great benefits of taking part in community worship is the potential for helping ourselves and others to keep our spiritual balance.

All these qualities may be present to a greater or lesser degree at times in our shouts of worship—we come to God with varying amounts of concentration, energy, faith, and enthusiasm. But we can always come to God seeking to express sincerely what our spirit holds.

WORSHIPING THROUGH RITUAL ACTIONS

We're accustomed to the idea of ritual in religion. But life in general also involves a whole tapestry of rituals that demonstrate our decisions and give form to the actions of our hearts. We marry. We graduate. We confirm. We induct. We divorce. We enlist. We baptize and inaugurate, retire and eulogize. Each of these rituals stands for a decision or a commitment, a beginning, a passage, or an ending. And through each we affirm to ourselves and others that we've reached a milestone. Our rituals contribute to our sense of what the milestone means in our life and communicate what we mean by it.

We engage in lesser rituals as well. We rise when a newcomer enters the room, shake hands to indicate greeting, ask a blessing before we eat, save certain days for particular activities, prepare traditional meals for certain holidays, and participate in certain holidays for particular remembrances. In these ways, we routinely celebrate, mark, and remember what we care about and who we are as individuals, families, a community, and even a nation.

Even on the most personal level, we find ritual ways to express deeper beliefs and relationships. My husband and I start our day before anyone else is up or the day's business has begun with a cup of coffee together. We always sit in the same place, and we have almost a litany of conversation that we repeat daily. Details change, but the topics tend to be the same. We establish how our day will proceed, catch each other up on the previous day, track the various members of our far-flung family, and talk through shared or individual concerns. In this way we manage both to honor our partnership and to keep communication open and productive.

Worship Through Ritual

HELPS US TO FOCUS

REMINDS US OF GOD'S PRESENCE IN OUR LIFE

GIVES US SYMBOLS TO EXPRESS SORROW

PROVIDES AIDS TO GRATITUDE

ADDS CLOSURE

When we seek God's presence alone, there will be moments of intense spontaneity, epiphanies, and surprises. But the habit of seeking God, like any worthy habit, will also include spells in which discipline alone keeps us going, without ecstasy or fireworks. In those times more than any other, ritual can help us to continue and grow in our search for God.

What do we hope for when we build ritual actions into our time with God? How do they serve our deeper longings and intentions?

❧ *First, they can help us to focus.* We may cover our heads or don a specific piece of clothing. Or we may light a candle or sit in a certain seat. We may recite a formal prayer or read a passage of Scripture. Ilsa, for example, reads her way through the Psalms regularly by making a part of a psalm the starting point of every time with God. In any of these and other ways, we signal that we are now "on holy ground." Our shoes are removed. We are ready to meet God.

❧ *Second, rituals can remind us of God's nature and activity in the world and our lives.* Biblical stories of Israel's early history tell of God instructing the faithful to place stones, build altars, and bestow specific names to places that will remind people of God's gifts and provisions. We may have our own God-centered moments to recall. We can gather small monuments and mementos of those times and events— photos, certificates, objects from nature, announcements, or printed services—that bring God's involvement in our lives to mind as we engage in intimate worship.

❧ *In addition, rituals can give us symbolic ways to express sorrow for our wrongdoing.* In modern culture, we often toss off slippery morality in ourselves and others—usually in the name of tolerance —with the statement "That's between me [or you] and God." Now, there's some virtue and a great deal of truth in this. But it loses its meaning, as well as its power toward forgiveness and fresh starts, if we never follow through with God. When we establish a ritual in our time with God specifically for confession, whether it involves writing things down or simply remembering and speaking, we make room in our spirits for healing and forward motion.

♯ *Rituals can also provide aids to gratitude.* We usually remember to ask for God's help. We often forget to notice when it comes. Personal thanksgiving rituals—that is, specific times and ways that we always include thanks—can bring us back to the Giver and keep us from the self-centered delusion that all good things are owed to us. This may be as simple as the habit of making a daily list of specific items we're thankful for that day.

♯ *Finally, rituals can provide a sense of closure.* In reality, we need never leave the presence of God, because God is Spirit and available at all times and in all places. Yet as we seek God, we find comfort and fuel for continuing when we know we have stood on holy ground for another day. Don always ends his time with God by reciting the same biblical benediction from Psalm 19: "May the words of my mouth and the meditation of my heart be pleasing in your sight, O Lord, My Rock and my Redeemer." Carol bows her way out of God's presence. "I think of God as the ultimate Royalty," she has told me. "It just seems right to me to show some serious respect." These are ways two people put their shoes back on, ways of saying, "Let me carry something holy from this time into the humdrum."

People respond differently to rituals. Sometimes we associate religious rituals so closely with religious institutions that we lose a sense of their value in our personal lives. But for many, simple rituals create a structure that encourages our seeking and build a sense of continuity that helps us get through the times when our spirits feel dusty and dull. They can also add beauty and form that bring us a closer sense of God's presence, especially as we continue to practice them through the ups and downs of our lives. The rituals become the temple or sanctuary we carry with us through the emotional and geographical changes that come in every lifetime.

One final note of encouragement: Anything we do routinely can eventually fall into the danger zone we call a "rut." When that happens, far from letting it rob the life out of our time with God, we can use it as a spur to be adventurous, to try new avenues of expression or find new ways to seek God's presence in our lives. Take a break from any routine that no longer serves. You may come back to it later, when it has had time to regain its power, or you may replace it with new rituals that better suit the new place in which you find yourself.

Worship flows out of a deep consciousness of God—it is our spirit's response in the presence of a loving Deity. Whether our worship takes the form of silence and meditation, overflowing exuberance, ritual actions, or a symphony of them all, we celebrate God at its center. The better we know God, the more natural and constant our worship becomes, until finally it becomes the exciting, energizing centerpiece of our life.

Meditations

ON INTIMATE WORSHIP

The following meditations and readings offer starting points for you to reflect on your own experience of worship in your time alone with God. Nowhere does our individuality make itself more apparent than in this time when we open ourselves to respond sincerely to the God who loves us. Give your reverence and exuberance free expression. If you find yourself feeling inhibited, take the time to identify what stands in the way of your honest, openhearted expression. Do what you can to eliminate it. Give yourself the opportunity to worship in different settings and in different ways. God welcomes our worship, and we blossom through it.

Day One

Good parents want their children to thrive, to be safe, to be moral, to be happy. They tend to disapprove of anything that gets in the way of these goals. But that disapproval in no way equals the end of love. So, too, with God, who may expect us to grow and change but who continues to love us, not because we are worthy but simply because we are.

When we worship, when we fix our attention on the One who is completely worthy of adoration and praise, we open the way for God to draw us toward a life that reflects all that is worthy, one in which we will flourish.

As you concentrate on God's attributes today, consider how those qualities can more fully infuse your life.

BIBLE READINGS

1 Chronicles 16:23-25   *Ephesians 4:1-6*

Day Two

*I*n *The Pursuit of God,* A. W. Tozer wrote: "Self is the opaque veil that hides the Face of God from us."

We live in a time when self-esteem and self-centeredness are often confused with each other. It's healthy to care about and for ourselves. But we can also get so caught up in ourselves and our own concerns that we have difficulty putting God at the center of our attention even for a short time. And we miss the wonderful opportunity to gain a clearer vision of the Divine.

Notice today the ways in which self-concerns may be a curtain of preoccupation between you and God.

BIBLE READINGS

Job 26:7-14   *1 Corinthians 13:11-12*

Day Three

At times, our spirits feel parched and dusty, like earth that has endured a drought. In those times, we can offer a special kind of worship—our quiet willingness to stand on holy ground despite our feelings. In such a simple way, we find ourselves in the right place to receive—like the dry earth receiving a soaking rain—the quenching, reviving presence of God.

Consider how you can worship with a quiet, ready spirit today.

BIBLE READINGS

Isaiah 57:15-19   1 Peter 5:6-11

Day Four

*I*n the natural world, every created thing has its own music:

The whisper of tall grasses.

The creak of tree branches.

The clapping of leaves and the clacking of stones.

The lap of soft waves and the thunder of breakers.

The chuckles and chatter, trills and caws, of beasts and birds.

The patter of rain and the soughing of wind.

All these are the songs God's creation lifts up to its Creator.

What is your song? Let yourself make a joyful noise
before God today.

BIBLE READINGS

Psalm 96   *Colossians 3:12-17*

Day Five

Reversing a familiar saying, the English poet Ralph Hodgson once wrote, "Some things have to be believed to be seen."

The Bible says that in the beginning God spoke all that exists into being: "God said, 'Let there be . . . ,' and there was. . . ." When we believe in the inestimable power of a single utterance spoken by God, we glimpse the Creator.

Focus today on belief in the Power who can transform nothing into something with a word.

BIBLE READINGS

Genesis 1:1-26   John 1:1-18

Day Six

God need not have blended so much predictability into the stew of surprises we call our universe. But this great and complex dance of cycles and seasons and repeating patterns is God's gift of hope to humankind. We know by it that sunsets lead to sunrises, winter to spring, and life to love.

Is there a part of your life today in which you need to remember the hope God offers?

BIBLE READINGS

Isaiah 40:28-31   1 John 3:1-3

Day Seven

When my children were in their early school years, I would occasionally pen a little note on the corner of the paper napkin I tucked into their lunch boxes. "Smile," I would write. Or "You are my sunshine." Or "Do you know how great you are?" That's all I wrote, but the children knew exactly what I meant: "I love you." "I'm thinking of you." "You can be sure I'm here."

God tucks a dozen "I love you" notes into every day of our lives. We only need to remember to read them.

BIBLE READINGS

Psalm 107:1-9   John 3:16-21

Shout for joy to the Lord, all the earth.
　Serve the Lord with gladness;
　come before him with joyful songs.
Know that the Lord is God.
　It is he who made us, and we are his;
　we are his people,
　the sheep of his pasture.
Enter his gates with thanksgiving
　and his courts with praise;
　give thanks to him
　and praise his name.
For the Lord is good
　and his love endures forever;
　his faithfulness continues
　through all generations.

Psalm 100

CHAPTER SIX

Dialogue With God

ATTITUDES *of* PRAYER

I GREW UP IN A PART OF THE WORLD THAT IS BLESSED WITH A HIGH WATER TABLE AND PLENTY OF PRECIPITATION. SO THE FIRST TIME I FLEW OVER ARID COUNTRY, I WAS MYSTIFIED BY THE OCCASIONAL RIBBONS OF GREEN THAT I COULD SEE, EVEN FROM 30,000 FEET IN THE AIR, WINDING ACROSS THE BROWN LANDSCAPE. A NATIVE OF THE AREA SAT BESIDE ME IN THE PLANE, AND I ASKED HIM WHAT EXPLAINED THE PHENOMENON. "OH, THOSE ARE just rivers," he said. "Only place anything grows green around here is by the rivers."

Water. Seventy-five percent of the human body is water. Roughly three-quarters of the globe's surface is water. Next to the air we breathe, our most urgent survival need is water. Fascinating, then, that biblical writers regularly compare the human connection to God with a direct link to water. The Psalmist, describing the person who makes God the subject of daily meditation, speaks metaphorically of a "tree planted by water." When the ancient tribe of Israel—who were following God as they fled from slavery in Egypt—camped in the desert, they were described as "gardens beside a river," "cedars beside the waters." And when Jesus identified himself with God, he declared to his audience, "If anyone is thirsty, let him come to me and drink." He referred to the divine connection he offered as "streams of living water."

In spiritual terms, worship is the act of breathing life-giving air, while prayer opens the channel through which life-giving water can reach us. Worship and prayer work together, spill over into each other; many times we don't know where one ends and the other begins. Nor do we need to know. In prayer, as in worship, we seek to come close to God. At times, prayer feels to me like digging a trench in the desert from where I am planted to the source of water. At other times, it seems more like making a little crack in a floodgate. Whatever the intensity of effort, it opens the path to God's presence and love.

Many people take their first tentative steps into prayer using rote recitations or making simple requests, either as children during religious training or as adults in search of help and understanding. When we return to prayer again and again over time, we come to believe—even to know—that God loves us and welcomes us, and our prayers take on a new fervor. We seek to love God in return. Eventually, we may find that far from trench-digging labor, our prayers become an open-armed, open-hearted dance into the presence of God.

Prayer is communication, and, as such, it has many forms. Some prayers are memorized from Scripture, read from a book of prayer, spoken in our own words, spoken through the words of others, or not spoken at all. Our prayers may change dramatically in style and content from day to day or over the course of a lifetime because we ourselves change, as do our circumstances and relationships, as does our understanding of God.

What specifically do we pray? People of faith through the ages have created a variety of models for prayer. But finally, they seem to boil down to roughly the same components: adoration and worship of God; recognition of our wrongdoing and our need for healing and forgiveness; thanks for God's presence and provision in our lives and in our universe; and requests for help, for assurance, for needs, for transformation.

St. Augustine wrote that "true, whole prayer is nothing but love." Thomas Merton described prayer as "a kind of hidden, secret, unknown stabilizer, and a compass, too." Kathleen Norris writes: "I have learned that prayer is not asking for what you think you want but asking to be changed in ways you can't imagine." Whatever the form or content, we pray to open the way for God to quench our thirst.

Attitudes of Prayer

IT USED TO BE A JOKE AMONG THE STUDENTS AT THE local university that we could find the worst communicators by looking at the communications majors in the Speech Department. They knew the theories and understood the mechanics, but all that information and form never seemed to translate into the lively, effective dialogue we might have hoped for. The mechanics of our prayer have their place, just as the mechanics of human communication have theirs. Like the rituals in worship, the forms and intellectual content of prayer can give us a structure that helps us to open the way for God's presence. At the heart of prayer, though, lies not the outward practice but the inner attitudes that drive us in God's direction and draw from us our sincerest response to God's presence.

Our attitudes are the posture of our thought and feelings toward something. We don't emerge from the womb with a fixed set of attitudes, as though they were the color of our eyes or the shape of our bones and written into our genetic coding. They develop in us as we grow and mature. They can change spontaneously in the context of our experiences or learning, or we can work to change them by applying our will, our understanding, and our intentions. I believe that we can assume responsibility for the "posture" of our prayers, and by doing so, we open the way for God's involvement in our lives all the more.

Please understand that I am not talking about the raw stuff of emotion or facts. I am referring to what we *do* with all of that, how we put it together, and what we build on it. We do well always to remember that our attitudes have a profound effect on our lives, our actions, and our well-being. One person discovers that he has a rare, debilitating disease—that's the fact. He is initially filled with fear, anger, grief, and loneliness—those are the feelings. He could move on to an attitude of despair that leads him to retreat from the loving support of others, give up on healing, and sink into bitterness and lethargy. But suppose, instead, that he acknowledges both the facts and the feelings but replaces despair with hope? Then he reaches out to friends for courage, seeks doctors who possess the expertise needed to help, actively participates in therapies, perhaps even gives what remains of a short-

Attitudes

JOY

GRATITUDE

PATIENCE

PERSISTENCE

CONSTANCY

ened life to helping others. Attitudes spell the difference. This is as true when we seek God in prayer as when we approach a relationship with another human being, take on a new task, accept a difficult challenge, or even confront a terrifying situation.

What are the attitudes, then, that undergird the seeker digging the trench toward the Source of living water? Among them, I believe, are joy and gratitude, patience, persistence, and constancy in our prayers. I want to consider what these lofty words really mean, how we can encourage them into our thoughts and feelings, and how we can nurture them into full, warm life.

PRAYING AS THOSE WHO HOPE *Joy*

What do we hope for? I can't imagine a more pertinent question for daily living. If we started every day with that thought and arranged our plans and attitudes accordingly, I wonder how different many of our lives would be. Hope pulls us out of the moment—with its complicated web of temporary highs and lows, goods and bads, successes and failures—and places us in a larger context. With hope, we carry in us both what exists and what is possible. We see simultaneously where we *are* and where we *can be* in the future. We live beyond the limits of time and space because our immediate experience does not define the potential.

When we seek God, hope reaches its ultimate expression. We extend the boundaries of what's possible into the realm of the eternal. Prayer, in fact, is hope in action, and the range of our hope in prayer has no known boundary. Why else approach God? We hope that we will be received, that we will be heard and answered. We hope that we will be loved and nurtured into our best selves. We hope as we dig the trench that the water will arrive and quench our spirit's thirst.

This God-centered hope is not wishful thinking, not a pie-in-the-sky optimism that denies reality. We build our hope on the real evidence in nature and in human life of God's presence and character. We build it on our instincts, both innate and developed over time, about God's good intentions for us. We hope as well on the basis of our own and others' experiences when we have sought God in the past. Out of hope grows joy.

I want to distinguish joy from happiness. I see happiness—a much-touted state in today's world—as almost always conditional. I'm happy when all goes well, when I get what I want, when the sun shines and soft breezes blow. The converse is also true. If I fail, run out of money, or lose a friend—if a storm breaks over my parade—happiness flees. *Joy*, as I'm using the word here, refers to a state of well-being and contentment that runs deep enough to survive the vicissitudes.

I think of Jean and Stephen, who work in a group home for children coming out of destructive living situations. Jean and Stephen encounter daily physical danger, discouragement, battles with bureaucracies, and uncertainty about continued funding for the home. Yet, even in the midst of the latest crisis, they devote themselves with love, energy, and goodwill to each new boy and girl who arrives at the home. How do they do it? "We look at the kids whose lives have turned around here," they tell me. "We know the same is possible for the new kids. We feel we're doing good, and we hope for more good even than we know about." Jean and Stephen often experience frustration about the progress of one child or another, but a strong undercurrent of joy sustains them. Their joy emanates from the steady hope of a good outcome.

Praying With Joy

PLACE GOD AT THE CENTER

OPEN YOURSELF TO A TRANSCENDENT PURPOSE

EXPECT AN ANSWER IN GOD'S TIME

Joy allows us to continue in the face of unhappiness. It gives us the wherewithal to rise above temporary setbacks. It transforms our daily experience so that our circumstances lose the power to control us.

How do we pray with joy? How do we pray as those who hope?

❧ *First, we place God at the center of our praying.* Remind yourself of Who it is you address in prayer—the Almighty, the Creator, the Sustainer, the Holy One. Our hope depends on God, not on ourselves, whatever our momentary condition or needs or thirst. God is not subject to our limitations, and the knowledge of this should fill us with the greatest of hope and the deepest of joy, if only we can appreciate its real significance.

☾ *Second, we open ourselves to taking part in a purpose that transcends ourselves.* It's comforting when life goes well. But when all that we can see looks grim or impossible, we can lose hope and the joy that hope produces. As you pray, remember that God has the whole picture, and you have a unique part in that picture, regardless of your ability to see what it is. You have only to cooperate in the process. God does the rest.

☾ *Third, we expect our thirst to be quenched in God's time.* Pay attention to the lessons of nature as you consider the life of your own spirit. All of God's creation has its cycles—times of growth and fruitfulness, seasons of rest, periods when moisture is plentiful, and others when roots have to sink deep to find it. The Psalmist writes: "Weeping may remain for a night, but rejoicing comes in the morning." God provides in the right way at the right time, if we only crack open that floodgate.

When we pray, it is our ultimate expression of hope: for a place in the larger picture that only God sees; for answers to life's dilemmas that only God can provide; for a direction that leads into the presence of the One who made us and can make our lives a song of joy.

PRAYING AS THOSE WHO DEPEND *Gratitude*

One of my favorite episodes of the old *Bill Cosby Show* culminates in a confrontation between the fictional dad, Cliff, and his oldest child, Theo. Theo has just outlined some grandiose scheme, and his father has responded that it would cost a great deal of money. "That's no problem," responds Theo. "We're rich!" Cliff turns to him (in Cosby's inimitable style) and declares, "Let's get something straight here. *You* [pointing to Theo] have nothing. *We* [pointing to himself and Theo's mother] have everything. *You* aren't rich. Your mother and I are rich."

I'd guess I'm not the only parent who enjoyed a moment's glee at that announcement, because I'm *sure* that I'm not the first or the last parent to deal with children who take the privilege and love in their lives for granted. Many times, children act as though lots of plenty plus a little bit more is their due.

The fact is, a child depends completely on his or her parents in the early years of life, and we do carry the responsibility of providing all that they need. A good parent has no interest in undermining a child's sense of safety and security; nor does that parent have any interest in withholding anything that is good for the child. I want my children to assume that they will have all they need from me, that they *can* depend on me because I love them. But I also want them at some point to realize how much they have received simply because they are loved, and to appreciate it. I want them to be grateful. Why? Because gratitude helps them to become better, more joyful people— people who can themselves love and forgive, who can give and receive in equal, generous measure, and who can find comfort and joy in the life they have been given.

In *Simple Abundance*, Sarah Ban Breathnach describes her own journey toward gratitude, beginning with the realization that abundance and lack are "parallel realities." "Every day," Breathnach writes, "I make the choice of which one to inhabit." When we seek God, we seek the One on whom we ultimately depend, the One who, finally, provides all the good in our lives, even life itself. We may choose to live in the "reality of lack," to concentrate our attention on all that we wish we were or had. To do that, however, is a great deal like turning up our noses at all the good our parents provided for our nurturing and well-being; like saying, "Well, sure you loved me and gave me food, clothes, shelter, an education, and big chunks of your life. But look at all this that you didn't give!" When we choose instead to focus gratefully on all that we are and all that we have been given through the grace of God, we create an opening in the wall of our self-absorption—a natural state in infancy, but an increasingly alienating condition as we mature—and it widens the conduit for God's loving presence and provision.

Consider what happens when we choose gratitude as our posture for prayer, when we say, "Okay! Let's see what you have in mind for me. I can't wait!"

Praying With Gratitude

WE GAIN A CLEARER VIEW

WE FREE OURSELVES TO ENJOY OUR TRUE RICHES

WE DISCOVER THE ABILITY TO GIVE

WE MOVE CLOSER TO THE GIVER

We gain a more authentic view of ourselves and others. As we express our thanks in prayer, we remember not only our dependence on God but our importance to God and, by extension, the importance of others. Such an awakening lies at the heart of maturity. We are saying: "I'm not the center of the universe, but I am a vital part of it."

We also free ourselves to recognize and enjoy our lives' true riches. Most of us know people who are never satisfied, who perennially believe that the next accomplishment, acquisition, or relationship will provide the happiness that seems to elude them. If, instead, we consciously, prayerfully, take note daily of the good in our lives, we can live joyfully today. The "what ifs" and "I wishes" in life can trap us to the point that God's goodness and provision are completely lost on us. What a waste! Today is what we have. Today we can live fully and joyfully.

In addition, we discover within ourselves a storehouse out of which we may give to others. The richest people I have met were not the ones with a lot of material assets. Rather, they were the ones who always had something to offer others out of the overflowing riches of their own spirits—a shoulder to lean on, a practical expression of sympathy in the form of a ride or a meal, a good belly laugh on a dark day, a thoughtful answer to a genuine question. What doodad that money can buy could ever compete with the outpouring of one heart to another?

Finally, we move closer to the Giver of gifts. When out of our gratitude we develop a giving spirit, we take a giant step in the direction of the Divine. The Psalmist praises God in this way: "But you, O God, do see trouble and grief; you consider it to take it in hand. The victim commits himself to you; you are the helper of the fatherless." I am convinced that many, many times, we are the hands God intends to use when others need help, and we act to that end in the context of gratitude.

PRAYING AS THOSE WHO TRUST *Patience*

When I took my first job as an editor on a magazine, I knew next to nothing about what I'd been hired to do. The man who hired me—who, incidentally, was well aware of my lack of experience—was also my boss. In the first weeks, I couldn't dog the man's steps closely enough for my own comfort. I knew what a distance I needed to cover to become effective in the job, and I felt certain that he could provide all the information I needed.

Somehow, though, he seemed less than willing to meet my expectations. I endured many silences while I waited for answers to my questions, and when he did answer, what he said often seemed only indirectly related to what I had asked. Many evenings, as I drove home from a long day's struggle with my responsibilities, I seethed with frustration at the boss. And I feared that I was getting nowhere.

But over time, I began to see evidence that I was becoming more skilled in my work. As I gained more confidence, I slowly, tentatively began to use the creativity that, I feel sure, had landed me the job in the first place. All the while, I continued to get to know the boss better. The longer I worked with him, the better I understood the way he worked and the more I came to appreciate him. I discovered in him a person of exceptional talent and integrity. And as I learned to trust him, I became a more patient learner. I realized that I could rely on him to prevent me from making some fatal mistake, and I saw more and more evidence that he knew what he was doing, whether he chose to answer my questions directly or instead let me learn on the job.

I look back on that experience now and see the wisdom of his approach. He gave me the fundamentals, but he left me largely on my own—with close supervision—to apply them to the particular tasks. He knew that simply to tell me what to do in each case would, in fact, short-circuit the learning process I needed to go through. I could have done the work exactly as he directed, but I wouldn't have known *why* I was doing it that way. The next time a task came up—in a job that demanded creative problem solving at all times—I would be just as clueless as I had been at first. Furthermore, because I lacked the experience to appreciate the whys and hows peculiar to the job, I would just as likely have resisted what he told me and learned the hard way.

We often turn to prayer when we don't understand some aspect of ourselves or our lives. We approach God because we aren't sure what to do next or because what we have done hasn't turned out well. Or we pray because we or someone else is in some sort of need and we hope that God will fix it. In all cases, we want answers, and for the most part, we want them now.

What we lose sight of at such times is that far more hangs in the balance at all times than the desires, pain, or confusion of our present moment. We experience in the moment, to be sure, but we take part in a universal, eternal reality. Sometimes God answers prayers immediately and obviously. But many times, we wait. The quality of our waiting can either limit our opportunity to grow and learn or open us to the best possibilities God has in store for us. Our lives play out against a far grander canvas than we can imagine or understand. We may sometimes have to wait for God's answer to our prayers because we aren't ready to receive the answer. Our character may need maturing; our mind may need clarifying; our spirit may need softening, healing, or refreshing.

When we seek God, we are in part looking for who God is so we know whether it's safe to invest our trust. As we come closer to the Creator and Sustainer of all that exists, we have the potential of finding the assurance that allows us to pray with patience. And we build that assurance by considering the particular aspects of God's being and what they mean to us right now. For example:

❦ *If we trust God's wisdom, we can wait without fear for illumination when we don't understand.*

🌿 If we trust God's goodness, we can take a positive, active role in moving through and beyond our hurts, no matter how long it seems to take.

🌿 If we trust God's power, we can let the unseen path ahead of us unfold as slowly as it must without losing heart.

🌿 If we trust God's love, we can engage in the lifelong adventure of love that grows and deepens only with time.

Patience is not a virtue in great favor today. We want and expect instant gratification. But, in fact, most of what has lasting value in this life and beyond takes time, with much uncertainty and a fair amount of challenge along the way. Patience is the response that allows us to stay with the process long enough to reap the rewards.

PRAYING AS THOSE LOVED *Persistence*

Persistence, the active twin of patience, takes us a little farther along the road of disciplined prayer. Just as we don't typically like to be kept waiting, we may find it difficult to keep returning to prayer when we've had to wait. We may be tempted to throw up our hands and say, "Forget it. I give up." But I cannot forget the metaphor of water. And if God is indeed the Source of our spiritual survival and health, I cannot readily give myself up to that arid place where God's provision goes ignored. So I ask the question: What keeps us coming back, even when we do not sense God's presence or see God's answers to our prayers?

I remember enjoying a long-ago holiday with a group of families who traveled to watch a well-known fireworks display. As we waited for the show to begin, my friend Gloria's young son started yanking on his mother's shirttail. "Can I have some cotton candy?" Michael asked, pointing to the concession stand, his eyes bright. His mother ignored him, but I could tell that Gloria was well aware of Michael's tugging. She was choosing not to respond.

After several tries, Michael's face took on a pensive look. I could see inspiration dawn, and I wasn't surprised when he finally gave another tug,

Praying as the Loved

RECONSIDER THE PURPOSE OF PRAYER

RETHINK YOUR REQUESTS

REMEMBER WHO IT IS YOU ARE ASKING

said "Excuse me," and repeated his request. Gloria turned to him, listened, then replied, "We can't get anything right now, Michael. The fireworks are about to begin." Michael's body stiffened up, and his chin jutted out. The fireworks soon distracted him, but as soon as they were over, he repeated his "Excuse me" and asked again with grim determination.

Gloria laid her hand on his head and smiled. "I don't want you to eat cotton candy," she said. "It's not good for you." Michael's jaw dropped in outrage. He'd been polite. He'd waited till the end of the show. And now the answer was no. "But I'm *hungry!*" he blurted out. Gloria squatted down so she could look her son directly in the eye. "Are you really hungry?" she asked. "Or do you want candy?" "I'm hungry *and* I want candy," he said. "Candy won't help your hunger," she answered. "But I'd be glad to get you a hot dog." In the end, after due consideration, Michael agreed to the hot dog.

What kept Michael coming back to his mother with his request, despite his frustration? First, his genuine hunger. He wanted the candy, but underneath that desire was real need. Beyond that, though, was his certainty that he could keep asking, and eventually they would come to an understanding of some kind. Past experience and a little boy's instincts told him that his mother loved him too much to ignore him or his real need.

God is Spirit, and when we pray, most of us never see a physical Presence or hear an audible Voice. But we have ample evidence around and in us of God's love. And we have the ability to reflect and learn and change. When God lets us wait, we can learn to trust in God's purpose for us. When God seems to say, "No," we can remember that we have a limited view of the whole picture, while God sees and understands it all. At the same time, we need never sit on our hands. We can participate in the fulfillment of God's purpose by persisting to approach the Almighty while we wait.

    When you see no answer to your prayer, reconsider the purpose of prayer. Could God want you to keep asking for a reason? Could there be some specific value for you right now in the process of waiting?

    When you see no answer to your prayer, rethink the request. Is it possible that what you want is not what you need? Could you be asking the wrong question? Can you imagine aspects of God's eventual answer that you cannot know? Have you considered the possibility that the answer is "Not yet" or even "No"?

When you see no answer to your prayer, remember Whom you ask. What are you learning about God as you persistently request an answer? What are you learning about yourself? What effect has the wait had on your perspective in general?

When we know we are loved, we can persist in approaching God because we know that we don't pray in vain.

PRAYING AS THOSE WHO LOVE *Constancy*

A wonderful transformation happens to people when they receive relentless love. Again, my friends Jean and Stephen at the group home come to mind. They have told me that the single most important element in their work with the children in the home is their genuine, constant love for those kids. That alone draws some of the children out of their traumatized past, teaches them how to love in return, and launches them into the possibility of healing and a healthy future.

Love allows us to be vulnerable enough to learn and grow. It gives us energy and lifts us out of ourselves. The prophet Isaiah describes those "who hope in the Lord," those who have experienced God's love and have loved in return, in this way: "They will soar on wings like eagles; they will run and not grow weary; they will walk and not be faint." Not only do we soar to the heights, we gain the stamina to continue and the ardor to be loyal.

We pray in the first place to open the way for God to quench our deepest thirst. We continue to pray when we experience God's love. We eventually long to pray when God's love teaches us to love in return. I have asked myself, in the quiet of my own heart, "How would I feel if God went away?" The desolation that follows such a thought is revealing. The joy and gratitude that come from knowing that God, in fact, will not go away give me patience and the ability to persist when my prayers seem to be greeted by silence. Further, they awaken a longing to pray that reflects and answers the love I've received.

How do we pray as those who love? We remember our Creator in all aspects of our lives. We develop the habits of turning to God, of trusting and leaning on God daily. And we listen ardently for that divine voice, we watch expectantly for that sacred movement in our lives, because it is a presence for which we long.

Meditations

ON PRAYER

*L*et the following thoughts and readings be an offering of encouragement as you consider the attitudes of prayer. If you are keeping a written record as you spend time alone with God, feel free to include both your prayers and your own meditations on prayer. Remember, God already knows all about you. You can pray with complete honesty and without fear. God wants to quench the thirst that prayer expresses.

Day One

Søren Kierkegaard once wrote: "Prayer does not change God, but it changes him who prays."

What a relief to know that God remains the unchanging foundation that supports and sustains every one of us and the universe that is our home. What a heart-lifting hope to realize that as we come to God—seeking to connect, to speak and be understood, to listen and understand—we don't have to remain exactly the same as we've been in the past. What is wonderful in us can be polished to greater beauty. What is limited can be expanded. What is wrong can be redeemed and remade.

Consider what in you has changed already in the presence of God. What changes do you hope for today?

BIBLE READINGS

Psalm 9:1-2   Hebrews 12:28-29

Day Two

*I*t's often amusing, even amazing, to hear two people each tell a story from their shared past. That people can be in the same place at the same time and experience the same situation, yet remember it in two very different ways, says a lot about how we experience our lives. Often it is more our attitude—the lens through which we see and experience— than it is the experience itself that dictates what we remember.

Joy can act as a strong lens in our life to bring into focus what is positive, good, and hopeful in our experiences. Prayer may teach us joy as we consider God's hand in every facet of our lives. And joy may infuse our prayers as we express the hope and certainty we feel. What lens most often filters your view of life? As you pray today, consider how God's presence in your life may adjust your focus.

BIBLE READINGS

Psalm 16:7-11   *1 Thessalonians 5:16-24*

Day Three

*I*t's tempting to worry about tomorrow's needs and forget what God has already provided for us today. When we learn to give at least as much attention to giving thanks for today as we do to planning for tomorrow, we begin to understand the nature of God's giving and the reality of our dependence. Without God, we would not exist. With God we can experience an abundance of spirit, mind, and body that transcends today's needs and tomorrow's possibilities.

Take time today to remember and give thanks for all that God has provided *for today*.

BIBLE READINGS

Proverbs 30:7-9   2 Corinthians 9:8-15

Day Four

When we plant a two-foot oak sapling, we don't expect a towering shade tree in the following season. In fact, if we know our trees, we understand that we will wait many years before we enjoy the full benefits of the oak's maturity. In the meantime, we can watch its growth with interest and enjoy the small but miraculous changes that the yearly cycle of seasons brings to transform it.

When we bring our fears and hopes, dismays and requests, to God in prayer, we sometimes forget that while some answers may arrive with the next rising of the sun, many others need time—God's timing—to appear. We want our sapling to become a full-grown shade tree overnight, and we forget to appreciate the subtle changes that are bringing us—inch by inch—what we've hoped for.

Reflect on the prayers for which you have not seen an answer. Could the answers even now be saplings God is growing in good time?

BIBLE READINGS

Psalm 40:1-3   John 15:1-8

Day Five

I wandered one afternoon into a village shop and found a collection of unusually lovely pottery. The potter herself was on the premises, and I eagerly plied her with dozens of questions about the brilliance and depth of the pottery's colors, the shimmer in the glaze, the raised designs, the contrasting tones.

I couldn't begin to explain all that she told me. But I came away with a clear impression. She achieved such loveliness through many stages, and especially through multiple firings of those glorious glazes in the kiln.

We want to rush our way to beauty, skill, and richness of character. The One who made us knows that our development needs time. It takes multiple journeys into the "fire." It requires painstaking attention to details. God is able and willing to bring us to full beauty. Our part consists not only in waiting but in persistently, prayerfully putting ourselves in the hands of the Potter.

BIBLE READINGS

Psalm 25:4-10   Luke 18:1-8

Day Six

The dictionary defines *prayer* as "an address to God in word or thought." Most of us have a loose, probably similar definition of our own. But prayer can far transcend "an address," especially when it comes from a heart struggling with hardship or a spirit overflowing with praise. Then prayer becomes an expression that emanates from the very center of our being.

When we refuse to give up because we believe in God's goodness and power, something as fundamental as the simple in and out of breathing may become an act of prayer. When we can't keep from radiating with joy because we love God, something as unintentional as a beaming smile may express our prayer.

In God's presence today, take time to give your voice a rest and let your heart speak.

BIBLE READINGS

1 Samuel 2:1-2   Ephesians 6:18

Day Seven

I once overheard a conversation in which a man struggling with what he referred to as a "besetting sin" asked his spiritual counselor why God didn't deliver him. "Every time I'm tempted, I pray, but God doesn't help."

"Part of your problem," the counselor answered, "may be timing. If you want to avoid the cookie, for example, you'd best pray before you put your hand in the cookie jar."

When we've done wrong, when our besetting weaknesses and self-centered habits are taking over, confessing and asking forgiveness form a central part of our prayers. When we seek to live differently, however, prayer on the subject needs to precede wrongdoing.

Consider those areas in which you need to ask forgiveness. Reflect on how "prior prayer" might become a more regular part of your dialogue with God.

BIBLE READINGS

Psalm 139:23-24   1 John 1:8-9

To you, O Lord, I called;
    to the Lord I cried for mercy:
"What gain is there in my destruction,
    in my going down into the pit?
Will the dust praise you?
    Will it proclaim your faithfulness?
Hear, O Lord, and be merciful to me;
    O Lord, be my help."

You turned my wailing into dancing;
    you removed my sackcloth
    and clothed me with joy,
that my heart may sing to you
    and not be silent.
    O Lord my God, I will give you
    thanks forever.

Psalm 30:8-12

CHAPTER SEVEN

Learning to Fly

WHEN *the* ROAD IS BLOCKED

THERE COMES A MOMENT IN EVERY GREAT ADVEN-
TURE STORY WHEN THE PROTAGONIST FACES THE
ULTIMATE OBSTACLE, ONE SEEMINGLY SO DIFFICULT AS
TO BE INSURMOUNTABLE. I THINK OF THE MOVIE *E.T.*,
THE STORY OF AN ENDEARING LITTLE ALIEN WHO IS
ACCIDENTALLY LEFT BEHIND WHEN HIS SPACESHIP HAS TO
DEPART EARTH IN A HURRY. ALTHOUGH BEFRIENDED AND
SHELTERED BY A FAMILY OF CHILDREN, E.T. LONGS FOR

his extraterrestrial home. Over time he weakens and eventually falls ill (from what we infer to be homesickness). At the same time, government agents and scientists who have been searching for the creature arrive and take captive the entire household where he's hiding. At just the moment when it looks like E.T. will die, his ship returns to Earth, miraculously reviving the alien and restoring hope to his young human friends.

Now comes the grand scene: the children riding furiously on their bicycles toward the alien spaceship—E.T. in one of the bike's baskets —and a veritable army of police and military vehicles in full chase. The inevitable happens. Just when the brave young troop of cyclists thinks they have eluded their pursuers, official cars pull out in front of them from all sides, barring every conceivable escape route. Is this the end? Is E.T. done for?

Not at all, for in the last second, E.T. imbues his rescuers with his otherworldly power, the bicycles rise from the asphalt, and the children soar right over the heads of their would-be captors. The first time my family watched the climax of this movie, my son (seven years old at the time) jumped to his feet and let out a victorious roar.

How often I've remembered that moment. Such a satisfying picture of overcoming, of literally rising above the thing that would keep us from what we most long for.

Life rarely plays itself out like a well-plotted, happy-ending fairy tale, of course. It seems that it's when we set a course for what matters most to us that we most often find our way blocked, and we cannot expect a magical solution to clear the way. We may not be confronted with some dramatic obstacle—we may find that our way forward is just a bit constricted or that the path has become too bumpy for comfort —but we nonetheless reach a point at which forward motion ceases. This can be true in our education, in our careers, in our relationships, in our longing for security, and in our service to others. And it can be true when we seek a connection to God.

We've considered many aspects of seeking God: finding the physical time and space to be alone with God; uncovering attitudes that help us in the search; finding God's many messages to draw us near; and developing the self-discipline to continue. We've looked at what it means to worship and how a dialogue with God can grow out of it.

But what if our plans don't work out as we thought they would? What if everyday upsets and complications make it difficult to follow the path toward God that we've chosen? What if we discover in ourselves attitudes and habits that consistently get in our way? And what about the times when life throws its worst punches, or when we lose heart? What do we *do* when the road to time with God is blocked?

Perhaps a heartwarming tale of an alien creature who made it possible to fly so appeals to me (and to many others as well) because it speaks in some mythic way to what we sense about the Divine and about our own spirits. Our days may be filled with evidences of how earthbound and limited we are, but every once in a while, we catch a glimmer of greater possibilities. We remember that reality consists of more than what we can perceive or understand, and even within ourselves lies potential beyond the ordinary. When we reach an impasse to fulfilling our longing for God, we begin to hope that flying may not be out of the question.

Flying Lessons

WHAT LIES AT THE HEART OF LEARNING TO FLY when the road is blocked? In the face of obstacles, no matter what their cause or configuration, one vital element makes the difference between being stopped in our tracks and continuing: the willingness to *accept responsibility* for going forward.

When I met with a group who were trying to make God a high priority in their lives, we each agreed that between our weekly meetings we would work on developing the habit of time alone with God. When we met, we encouraged one another by sharing our experiences of the prior week. But one member of the group, Walt, arrived week after week only with stories of how frustrated he was in all his attempts—how put upon by family, how beset with work stresses, how beleaguered by a variety of mechanical breakdowns, ailing relatives, difficult neighbors. Over time, the group reached their limit with Walt's unending tale of woe. Finally one evening, another group member, Joan, turned to Walt and said, "Why don't you just *deal* with it, Walt. We *all* have problems. You're not *unique*, you know."

In the conversation that followed Joan's outburst, story after story emerged of the many roadblocks people faced daily while trying to maintain the discipline of time with God. The Walts of the group often allowed themselves to be the victims of whatever was getting in their way; but the Joans rose to the occasion, convinced that it was up to them—and that it was possible—to find a way to maintain their commitment.

In every case, it was attitude rather than the nature or seriousness of the obstacles that made the difference. Some said, "Well, sure, *you* keep going, but you're only dealing with a transmission problem. I'm caring for my sick father." But then we considered the lives of people such as Viktor Frankl *(Man's Search for Meaning)* and Corrie Ten Boom *(The Hiding Place)*. Those courageous souls faced some of the worst life can produce in the German concentration camps of World War II. In both cases, they described how they and others continued to call on

The Roadblocks

FALLING ROCKS

BARRIERS WE BUILD

WASHOUTS

BREAKDOWNS

God, in one way or another carving a place for the Eternal out of the most devastating of temporal circumstances.

In fact, it is in those most trying times that our connection to God may be most precious to us. We practice for the worst times when we take responsibility for overcoming the daily, minor obstacles that would keep us from seeking God. Like fledglings perched on the edge of the nest, we try our wings in small ways so that when we need to, we can soar above the barriers toward spiritual growth and connectedness. The more we know about what is getting in our way and why we find it an obstacle, the better equipped we become to "deal with it" wisely and effectively. Over time, the act of refusing to be stopped lends strength to our intention to faithfully seek God. We learn to fly.

FALLING ROCKS *Everyday Obstacles*

Through the rugged mountains of the western U.S., roadways often seem to be carved out of solid vertical granite. And all along the routes, signs declare the ever-present danger of falling rocks. The rocks can vary in size; they can fall singly or in minor avalanches. However they happen to come down, they bear watching because they clutter the way forward and can present the unwary with serious hazard or, at best, delay. Since driving those mountain roads, I've come to think of the many ordinary complications that clutter our lives as falling rocks. They can throw us off course, slow us down, bruise us, and sometimes stop us in our tracks. As we continue to seek God, we need to be less surprised so we're better able to respond productively. Identifying falling rocks in advance can help us plan what to do when they land in our path.

Take, for example, unexpected changes in routine.

Say we've found what seems to be the best daily time for focusing on God, and we've begun to establish a regular habit. Suddenly a family member gets sick and needs care. Or a friend's car breaks down and he needs the favor of a ride for a week; or a couple's marriage is breaking down and they need the favor of a listening ear for the duration. The furnace quits. The basement floods. The car overheats. The computer crashes. There's no avoiding these interruptions. They happen to every-one; in my experience, they often occur in multiples—little avalanches that throw our best-laid plans into a muddle.

Sometimes we *plan* the changes in our routine.

We take a vacation. We head out on a business trip. A baby is born. Out-of-town guests arrive. Usually, these changes happen at intervals with stretches of time between them. We consider them the bonuses of life; we look forward to them. The fact that they break up life-as-usual is part of their virtue. But they can nonetheless make it difficult to maintain the parts of our routine that we want to continue.

As well, we face glitches from within the time we plan for God.

We've built a ritual of place and action, perhaps, and then something falls *out* of place. We're out of coffee for that important cup to wake us up or keep us alert. We've somehow misplaced our Bible or the commentary we were using or the prayer journal we're keeping. We develop a headache. We notice that the chair we're sitting in is beginning to break. These "falling rocks" need not disrupt our time with God, but if they catch us on the wrong day, they make handy excuses to put aside discipline and break a growing habit.

In addition, we may face opposition from others to the time we've kept apart for God.

When we set a course for ourselves, it inevitably has some impact on the people who are closest to us. Even when we engage in a practice that does us only good and no harm to others, we may still find family members or close friends who are not sympathetic, who resent the time taken from them, or who simply feel left out. We may encounter anger in someone who does not share our longing for or belief in God.

Or we may find others reacting negatively to changes they perceive in us. Whether it comes from our spouse or life partner, parent, child, roommate, or best pal, this kind of obstacle can leave us feeling confused, disappointed, or even defeated.

The way past falling rocks of whatever sort begins with a proactive attitude. Rather than view ourselves as victims of the latest hurdle, we consider the challenge in terms of what we can do about it. The everyday variety of roadblock requires flexibility and patience. Happily, these states of mind and heart can be developed with exercise and serve us well for a lifetime, especially with regard to the Divine connection we hope for.

How can we go about building these attitudes?

We can accept flexibility and patience as viable choices. The next time you hear yourself say, "Well, so much for time with God today. It's blown," stop and reconsider. Such a statement reveals a *decision to give up.* The choice to wait and see what alternatives may exist, and the choice to try the alternatives, is just as available and a lot more satisfying.

We can look for creative adjustments to our routine. In the group I mentioned earlier, Joan told us that she tries out different times and places for God, even though she has found a time when she can almost always be alone to reflect and pray. "It's a little like going on scouting expeditions," she explains. "I experiment. That way, when my regular routine is messed up, I already have other ideas that I know will work."

✻ *We can approach disruptions as "speed bumps" instead of roadblocks.* That is, we can choose to slow down rather than stop altogether. Time with God every other day, maybe, or once a week, may not be as fruitful as time every day, but it still offers an ongoing connection to the Divine, as well as a pathway back to a more regular practice.

✻ *We can look for ways in which the interruption itself may offer an opportunity to approach God differently.* Mitch, a young man I know, told me about a time when his wife's sister came for an extended visit. With young children and a houseguest, Mitch found himself displaced for his prayer and meditation. Finally he decided to start his day with coffee at the corner deli. He felt too self-conscious to take his Bible or bow his head, habits he maintained at home. "Sitting in that restaurant with my eyes wide open, surrounded by people and in view of traffic," Mitch said, "having to be quiet and attentive from the inside out—it was a new experience. I've never felt closer to God than I did then."

✻ *We can learn to be positive opportunists.* It takes patience to wait for opportunities. It takes flexibility to grab them when they come along. And it takes a firm grasp of our priorities to set lesser plans aside when we've had to alter our discipline of time with God. Watch for the unexpected half hour between commitments. Excuse yourself from the evening news. Opt for a lunch on your own instead of with the usual group from work. Sometimes we don't see opportunities simply because we're not looking for them.

We can learn to negotiate. You probably did this when you first made time with God a part of your daily life. But human relationships and people's feelings are never taken care of once and for all. New resistance can arise in others after a time. When it does, we often need to search behind the obvious to discover what's really bothering them. When someone close to you is making it difficult for you to keep your commitment to God, ask that person this: "What do you feel is being taken from you when I give time to God?" It may be time and attention that's at issue, and you can renew the offer of trade-off time discussed earlier. It may be a sense of intimacy that's at stake. In that case, just the act of asking the question and then offering an explanation about why the time with God has become important to you can make the other person feel close and loved. Deeper antagonisms can grow in the face of differing beliefs, of course. In such a situation, it's vital not only to your own choices but to the health of the relationship to seek the help of a counselor or therapist in developing mutual respect and tolerance between you and that other person.

The first step toward dealing with the falling rocks in life is to acknowledge their existence. Take the time to understand the nature of

To Overcome Everyday Obstacles

CHOOSE FLEXIBILITY AND PATIENCE

LOOK FOR CREATIVE ADJUSTMENTS

VIEW ROADBLOCKS AS "SPEED BUMPS"

APPROACH GOD IN NEW WAYS

BECOME A POSITIVE OPPORTUNIST

LEARN TO NEGOTIATE

their power over you and your life. Question your assumptions about what is possible and try a variety of solutions that allow you to continue purposefully seeking God.

BARRIERS WE BUILD *Do-it-yourself Roadblocks*

While many barriers to time with God come from outside ourselves, there are others that we erect from within. They sound something like this: "I'm too busy today"; "I'm not in the right mood"; "I'm too tired"; "It can't be good for me to get up this early [stay up this late]"; "Nothing seems to be happening"; "God isn't making my life better/easier/happier"; "God isn't fixing this situation/this person/this pain."

When we talk to ourselves in this kind of language, we are often dealing with long-term habits of thought.

We managed to put aside such habits when we first started on the path toward God. But then we settled into a routine, and with routine has arrived some of our old, automatic reactions. We revert to old ways of thinking about the discipline the search requires, and we lose the stamina to continue. This process resembles what happens when we fall in love and then settle down. At first, nothing is too hard, no obstacle too great, in building our relationship. But when the first flush of infatuation recedes, we have less patience in the face of problems, less energy when the relationship requires an extra measure, less willingness to transcend our weariness or distractions or self-concerns.

We may also be dealing with a case of genuine overcommitment.

Every day really does consist of only 24 hours, yet many of us seem to forget that. We have unrealistic expectations of ourselves and of what we can accomplish. We say "yes" one too many times, without reference to the relative importance of the various activities, people, or responsibilities attached to each yes. Suddenly we are overloaded, and something has to give. Even when we long to know God, the time we've established for that connection can look like the easiest element in our day to dispense with because eliminating it presents no inconvenience to others. We "love others" to the point that we neglect the greatest means of loving ourselves.

We may expect a straight, upward climb in our spiritual life when we begin to seriously seek God.

We forget that growth is never a steady process. Think of adolescence, when we alternated between gawkiness and pudginess, euphoria and despair. We took on the appearance of an adult yet readily swung back into the emotions of our childhood. We went for months without growing a quarter of an inch and then suddenly sprouted half a foot in a single summer. The growth of our spirit can be just as uneven and confusing as the growth of our bodies, emotions, and intellects. The gap between what we expect and what we experience leaves us discouraged and sometimes even angry.

The barriers we build ourselves can be dismantled, if we are willing to face them honestly. As we identify self-constructed roadblocks, we can take positive steps to reinvent the habits, choices, and reactions that have stopped us on the path to God.

❧ *We take the primary step around these barriers when we refuse to ignore God.* Far from letting God be the first commitment we drop, we can turn to God for help in keeping that vital search at the heart of our life. One student told me that every time it occurs to him to cut God out of his schedule, he prays, "Help me to figure out what *really* should change." He says he has never failed to find a way when he has approached the problem with this prayer.

❧ *We further dismantle our self-made barriers when we learn to accept our own limits.* This may mean saying "no" more often. (You can say "no" sometimes—and it gets easier with practice.) It may mean sitting down with a schedule or calendar and being ruthlessly honest about how much time we have and what (other than God) needs to be eliminated. It certainly means accepting the fact that we're flesh and blood and require regular rest, reflection time, and revitalization. We can't do it all. We need to stop planning as though we can.

🌿 *We also help ourselves to continue seeking God when we accept our own seasons.* Just as we grow and change at an uneven pace, so does the thirst that drives us to God differ from time to time. To live in harmony with the seasons of our spirit and still actively seek a vital connection with God, I believe we need a gardener's sensibility. A gardener does not stop gardening when the growing season ends but, rather, plans and orders seeds and plants, starts the spring plantings indoors, begins to clear beds. Every season has its emphasis, but the garden is never out of mind or heart. When we're seeing change and sensing God's closeness, we can revel in it and give thanks, like a gardener in seasons of blossom, fruit, and harvest. When we seem to be dormant, we can trust the One we are seeking and exercise the discipline to keep going, making the winter of our spirit a time for study and quiet reflection.

WASHOUTS *Life's Major Disruptions*

Certain crises arise in every human life, if we live long enough. People close to us are taken by death or separation. Our deepest relationships slip into estrangement, or we divorce. We move, or we lose our home or our job. We or someone close to us contracts a chronic or terminal illness. Or we are suddenly faced with the unexpected birth of twins, a promotion that changes our life, a success that snowballs into unforeseeable activity. The predictable shifts in life can feel like crises as well: from childhood to independence; from school to employment; from employment to retirement. When these circumstances arrive, they can as easily draw us away from seeking God as send us in God's direction.

There is no antidote to the tough and challenging times of life —if there were, someone would have patented it and become very rich. There are only next steps and lives that go on, fear and tenderness, courage and hope. But we need not go into these times without a foundation that can hold us up in their midst. Instead, we can recognize the inevitability of washouts in every human life, and we can prepare.

❧ *Before the crises come, we need to deal honestly with the heavy stuff of life.* We can look at the potentials head-on, read up, take courses, find sources of wisdom in our elders, our pastors, and the people who deal with these crises as support providers. As we gather information and understanding, we can carry what we are discovering into the presence of God for reflection that reaches beyond our heads to our hearts.

❧ *When the crises arrive, we need to accept our feelings.* We can know that these circumstances and our reaction to them are part of our humanness. The more courage we muster to be honest in the midst of life's major disruptions, the more we can offer our emotions to God for healing and resuscitation.

❧ *We can seek human help.* Many people have found crucial assistance and the strength to go on in times of stress and crisis through a variety of support groups, through wise friends, spiritual counselors, and therapists. Never think that seeking or receiving help from other people means you've given up on God. Many times, God's answer to our needs comes to us in part through the agency of other people. We can offer thanks to the Almighty for every kind of help we receive because, ultimately, it is all from God's hand.

BREAKDOWNS *Our Private Pain*

Perhaps no more difficult barriers exist than crises of heart and faith. Many of us will experience one form or another of spiritual breakdown before our journey toward God is over. We will be overcome by doubts or fears. We'll sink into a season of depression or bitterness or anger. Or we'll wake up one morning and find a core of guilt or coldness in ourselves toward God.

In some cases, these barriers develop in the wake of external circumstances. A close friend of mine, after losing her young husband and child in an automobile accident, turned her back on God for a time. Her anguish and bewilderment over so terrible a loss left no room for the faith that had drawn her to seek God for most of her life.

At times, we find it hard to come to God because we are overcome by a consciousness of our wrongdoing. We feel as though God couldn't accept or forgive us because we can't or won't accept or forgive ourselves.

Such barriers can grow as well out of legitimate intellectual questions that focus on such enigmas as the presence of evil and suffering, out of unresolved emotional issues, physical exhaustion, even imbalances in our body's chemistry. Or they can develop when the pileup of events or challenges grows too high. At a recent period of my own life,

When Faith Breaks Down

REMEMBER
GOD'S MERCY

SEARCH OUT THE
PROMISES OF GOD

STUDY OTHERS'
SPIRITUAL JOURNEYS

TURN TO OTHERS
FOR SUPPORT

when it seemed as though crises confronted me on every side, there was more than one morning when I thought, "I don't have the energy to go to God. I can't even think, and I don't dare feel."

At just that point, a dear friend passed along a folk saying she had stumbled upon: "When you get to wit's end, remember that God lives there." It was a timely reminder in more ways than one. It helped me to face my feelings, and it helped me put them in perspective. It gave my "wings" a little shake-out. Instead of choosing to give up, I remembered the alternative and took responsibility for *what I did* about how I felt.

What alternatives are available to us when our spirit breaks down on the path toward God?

✻ *First and foremost, we can throw ourselves on God's mercy.* The psalmist writes, "Praise be to the Lord, for he has heard my cry for mercy. The Lord is my strength and my shield; my heart trusts in him, and I am helped." We sense in his song someone who could do nothing more than cry out. A prayer as simple as "Help me, please" is as true a prayer as the most eloquent, carefully composed psalm. An honest expression of what has stopped us flat can be brought to God as surely as a song of praise. Sometimes it is only at the end of our own strength, wit, and hope that we truly experience the greatness, forgiveness, and unlimited love of the Almighty.

We can search out the promises about God in Scripture. The sacred texts often seem to come most alive when we are deepest in pain. Before you experience the breakdowns in your spirit's life, comb Scripture for all that it reveals about God. Write down what you find. Read it aloud. Commit it to memory. In the midst of trouble, focus on who God is. When my friend Emily suffered her darkest hours after losing her eyesight, part of the road back into God's presence was paved with the Scripture she had memorized.

We can acquaint ourselves with the spiritual journeys of others. Every library and bookstore carries biographies and memoirs of people whose faith has been tested and proved. Their stories offer us glimpses into the real-life experiences of people who faced life's direst challenges and whose connection with God taught them to fly when the obstacles seemed insurmountable. In these stories we see ourselves and our own struggles, and through them we gain hope and courage to continue.

Finally, we can turn to others for support. The time may come when you find within yourself no further resources with which to reach toward God. You may not even be able to pray. At such a time, we can be thankful that we don't exist in a vacuum. God has made us part of the human community. When we've sputtered to a complete stop, we can call in reinforcements. We can ask others to pray on our behalf. We can make a spiritual counselor or pastor aware of our pain. Within the shelter of that support, we can face our feelings honestly and begin the journey back to God on the wings of others.

If you find that days, weeks, or months go by without time for God; if you feel as though you're dragging yourself into God's presence; if you realize that you're simply going through the motions without a sense of life and light—consider the possibility that you have encountered a spiritual roadblock. Give it a name. Accept responsibility for what you can change. Pray for patience and hope about what you cannot change. Ask forgiveness for attitudes or actions that may have turned you away from God. Wings sprout as we seek creative ways to turn once more in God's direction. And we feel the lift under those wings as we choose to begin again.

Meditations

ON LEARNING TO FLY

*T*he old adage that anything we continue for six weeks becomes a habit has proven true for many. In this, your seventh week of regular time alone with God, you can begin to build expectations about a lifetime's practice that will give you an ever-increasing number of flying lessons to draw upon. Make a record of the barriers you've encountered over the past six weeks. Then take the following meditations and Scripture readings to your time with God and let them give strength to your ever more dependable wings.

Day One

One day, as I worked in the highest tier of a terraced garden, my cat approached from the bottom. He stared across two tiers of shallow beds and a small fence that separated us. He meowed. "You'll have to wait," I answered. He meowed again, more insistently. "I'm not coming to get you," I said, and kept working. But out of the corner of my eye, I watched him pace, crouch, meow, and pace again. Finally, he hunkered down, did the feline pouncing dance, let out one more determined cry, and leaped the entire distance to my side. I hadn't known he could do that. If I were to read his behavior in human terms, I'd say he didn't know it, either.

Consider the obstacles in your way toward God. Could they be God's tutorial for a flying lesson?

BIBLE READINGS

Psalm 121:2-8   Ephesians 3:14-21

Day Two

$\mathcal{A}$ detour off the main path can give us a bigger view of where we are. It can familiarize us with alternative paths to where we want to go. It can teach us to plan ahead and keep us from taking too much for granted. And sometimes a dam is also a bridge.

Reflect on the roadblocks that you confront today. What detours might God have prepared to carry you forward in a new way?

BIBLE READINGS

Proverbs 20:20-27   Romans 11:33-36

Day Three

The American hotelier Simeon Ford once said, "If the Scotch knew enough to go in when it rained, they would never get any outdoor exercise." The implication, of course, is that the Scotch know enough *not* to go in when it rains; otherwise, they would make their life a smaller, less healthful, and less satisfying one.

Sometimes we hurry away from life's rainstorms—we get off the roads that seem blocked—because we "know enough" to avoid the trouble they involve. The question is, what do we miss in the process?

In God's presence today, look at those challenges in your life that tempt you to run away. What might God be offering to you if you choose differently?

BIBLE READINGS

Psalm 94:12-13   Luke 6:46-49

Day Four

Some time ago, an older couple who were friends of mine received within weeks of each other a diagnosis of terminal illness. After that time, they laid aside many lesser plans in order to spend time with family, to see a great number of old friends and colleagues, to throw a reception that gave them and the people they cared about a chance to celebrate shared lives. Of their situation they said, "Neither of us can imagine living without the other. We couldn't have planned this better."

If you knew that today were your last day on Earth, what are the things you would lay aside? What would matter most to you?

BIBLE READINGS

Psalm 39:4-5   *Romans 13:8-14*

Day Five

The window in my study is graced by the web of a large, fat spider. In the morning after a heavy wind, I find the lovely net tattered and incomplete. By noon the spider has repaired it and has already caught another day's meal. The spider seems unfazed by the impermanence of her day's work. She simply repeats it as often as need be. She doesn't know the fine job she's doing in pest control or the beauty she has contributed to my life.

Are there unavoidable aspects of your life that you find difficult to carry out faithfully? Consider the ways in which God might use your patient willingness for your good and the encouragement of others.

BIBLE READINGS

1 Chronicles 28:9-10   *1 Thessalonians 5:12-15*

Day Six

We should never forget the possibility that the way forward is blocked because we are not really through with where we are.

God can use the hard and painful places for our good. And sometimes we are not yet ready, not yet ripe, for what lies ahead. Take time to consider the ways in which tough times in the past have prepared you in positive ways for the future. Reconsider those aspects of your life that frustrate you in your pursuit of God.

BIBLE READINGS

Isaiah 30:20-21   Romans 5:1-5

Day Seven

I recently read about a region that had received so much rain over such an extended period of time that rivers and reservoirs threatened to flood and destroy acres and acres of property and disrupt many hundreds of human lives. Eventually, the rain ended. The rivers and reservoirs crested and began to recede without the extreme flooding that had seemed inevitable. Upon searching out what had spared the region, scientists discovered a series of enormous beaver dams along a critical path of watershed. Apparently, throughout the deluge, the beavers had worked nonstop to shore up their dams and protect their lodges against a devastating washout. In the process, they had saved their human neighbors from great loss as well.

Consider the elements in your present life that seem to be in your way. Could they have a purpose that serves your good?

BIBLE READINGS

Psalm 145:17-19   2 Corinthians 4:16-18

But the eyes of the Lord
are on those who fear him,
on those whose hope
is in his unfailing love,
to deliver them from death
and keep them alive in famine.

We wait in hope for the Lord;
he is our help and our shield.
In him our hearts rejoice,
for we trust in his holy name.
May your unfailing love
rest upon us, O Lord,
even as we put our hope in you.

Psalm 33:18-22

CHAPTER EIGHT

Transformations

The NATURE of OUR CHANGES

SOME 60 YEARS AGO, A STORM OF MIND-NUMBING PROPORTIONS RACED UP THE EASTERN SEABOARD OF THE UNITED STATES, POUNDING INTO THE NEW ENGLAND COAST WITH SUCH FURIOUS SPEED AND SO LITTLE WARNING THAT INHABITANTS WERE LITERALLY STOPPED, EVEN SWAMPED, IN THEIR TRACKS. BY THE TIME THE STORM ABATED—BUT NOT BEFORE IT HAD DELIVERED EXTREME WIND GUSTS OF ABOVE 180 MILES AN HOUR AND A STORM surge that measured 25 feet—680 lives had been lost. One observer declares, "The face of New England had been changed forever"; another, that "nothing was ever the same again after the hurricane."

The village in which I live was among those hit head-on by that disaster, and the 60th anniversary of the storm's occurrence inspired a great deal of local news coverage and watering-hole discussion, accompanied by the resurrection of old photos and the retelling of old tales. I wouldn't label it a "celebration." It was more like a solemn remembrance of a life-transforming event. When old-timers spoke of those who lost their lives, they referred to them in terms of their descendants, those who survived and carried on and rebuilt, those who learned lessons and gained perspective. Alongside the tragedies, their stories revealed, miracles of renewal took place.

I suspect that part of the strange and lasting power the hurricanes of life hold for us, both in community and as individuals, reflects a human longing for positive change, for growth, for a profound transformation. When we seek God, we stretch toward the ultimate source of transformative power. Yet while we long for transformation, we also fear it. We understand that with change may come losses. We may have to endure the storm before we make the new beginning. What we need to remember, I believe, is that life does not exist in the absence of change. When we choose to seek God, we choose to embrace change and growth—to be transformed.

The Nature of Our Changing

WHEN MY PARENTS BUILT THE HOUSE IN WHICH they would raise their family, they planted an apple tree in the backyard. That tree held a particular fascination for me as I grew up. An old apple orchard was located near our house, so I had a clear picture of what our own little tree would eventually become. For the first few years, of course, it looked nothing like the mature trees in the orchard. Its trunk was no thicker than my leg, and its upper branches were hardly taller than my father. It didn't burst into blossom in the spring. It produced no fruit in the fall.

In time, though, the first few blossoms began to appear. The tree gained enough height that Dad had to use an extension pole to prune the upper branches. In full leaf, the tree created a dappled pool of shade on a sunny day, and it offered a handful of perfect rosy-green apples come picking season. We developed a history with the tree. We began to notice correlations between weather conditions from year to year and the quality and abundance of the tree's yield. We mourned the loss of a branch after a storm and watched the tree sprout suckers in response. We noted the twist of the trunk as it followed some mysterious inclination of its own having to do with the direction of sun and wind, the amount of moisture in the ground, the level of pruning it received.

One year, the leaves showed spots, and as the fruits developed, they grew into oddly dimpled, misshapen orbs. The tree doctor, as we called her, informed us that our apple tree was under pest attack and needed spraying. We did what we were told, and by the next year, we were harvesting healthy fruit again. The tree produced so many apples that year, my mother had to prop some of the lower branches with sturdy poles to keep them from breaking under the weight. By the time I was bringing my own children for harvesttime visits, we could press fresh cider from the abundant windfall at season's end.

How We Change

NEW EYES

NEW HEART

NEW HANDS

I live far away now, my parents have moved, and I don't often visit the tree. But I intend to be there if the tree ever has to be taken down. I want a slice of the trunk, with its ringed record of a history I shared. In it I expect to see a picture of the tree's natural maturation. But I'll also see its periods of exceptional transformation: during unusually good weather conditions, after special care, in the wake of pests or storm or drought. And perhaps in it I'll remember as well my own growth and transformations.

Along with the normal process of maturation, life has a habit of throwing extraordinary situations at us—griefs to bear, joys to celebrate, traumatic changes to survive, opportunities to seize—our pests and storms, good seasons and special care. When we put ourselves on the path that leads toward God, we make it possible for the Creator to take all of the material of our lives and through it to shape us in a remarkable way. It doesn't surprise me that one of the many images Bible writers employed to describe the way God relates to us is that of the gardener lovingly tending his plants, or that human activity that reflects a close connection with God is often referred to as our "fruit."

I'm grateful for the hurricanes of life that awaken our desire for deep changes and new beginnings. I think perhaps they help us lay aside our fears and reluctance so we can willingly, courageously, open ourselves to transformation. And I'm glad for the apple trees in our experience—those graceful living pictures all around us of the many ways and time frames in which transformations occur. Together, the hurricanes and apple trees tell me that in God's care we may experience what people through the ages have termed enlightenment—a clarification of our spiritual sight and understanding.

NEW EYES *Enlightenment*

I'd like to dwell a moment more with my apple tree. When I was quite young, I used to lie on my back in the grass under the tree and watch how the sunlight shone right through the leaves so that the veins and stems became dark patterns on a light green field. At that time, I had no notion of photosynthesis. I didn't know that the light allowed the tree to nourish itself. I didn't know that the light let the tree take the used air I breathed out and turn it into oxygen for me to inhale. Nor did I know that without light the tree would soon die. It never occurred to me that if I'd first encountered the tree in absolute darkness, I would have had no idea what it looked like.

We begin our life with extremely limited vision. Our eyesight sharpens and clears in a relatively short time. But a true perception of reality—of who and what we are, of how we fit into the world around us, and of how all that we perceive fits together and makes sense—takes a lifetime. Theorists in cognitive development note that humans spend their first months just discovering that an object continues to exist when it is out of our view. We take years to realize that we don't actually occupy the center of the universe, with everything and everyone orbiting around us and our needs.

With New Eyes

A NEW VIEW OF GOD

A NEW VIEW OF OURSELVES

A NEW VIEW OF OTHERS

Even with maturity, we have limits to our ability to "see." We may understand we're just one of billions of human lives with attendant needs, hopes, and cares. But we may not be able to sort out our own life and we cannot foresee our future. We can only define reality in terms of what we know and understand, even when we "know" how much we *don't* know.

In the beginning, according to the Bible, God created the heavens and the earth. Then followed God's first creative words: "Let there be light." Until the existence of light, the earth had not been visible, and life as we know it had not been possible. But with the advent of this revealing, life-giving phenomenon, the work of creation could continue, and all the rest of what would ultimately make up the universe could unfold. When we are granted enlightenment—what I'm calling "new eyes"—what was formerly unseen is made visible. What was murky becomes clearer. What had no form takes on life and meaning.

We cannot see light; we can only see what it illuminates. God, who is Spirit, is invisible, but when God illuminates our view, we see the Divine in the visible.

First, we begin to develop a new view of God.

I once took part in a discussion of faith in which a number of us considered the question: "How do you see God?" One woman described the way that the biblical language of "God, the Father" had affected her perception. "My father was disturbed and sometimes abusive," she told us. "For the longest time, whenever I thought about God, I imagined an unpredictable, punitive Daddy threatening me in some way." It wasn't until someone shared with her the many other "names" that Scripture applies to God—terms that reveal numerous other aspects of how God relates to us—that she realized how limited her view of God was. She began to use her prayer and meditation time to simply reflect on God's being.

At the heart of seeing God more truly is our authentic desire to do so. In the first book of Chronicles, the Bible records King David's prophetic words to his son Solomon: "Acknowledge the God of your father, and serve him with wholehearted devotion and with a willing mind, for the Lord searches every heart and understands every motive behind the thoughts. If you seek him, he will be found by you. . . ." If we want our spiritual sight to be transformed, we first put ourselves in a place in which God can be found by us. For example:

Make the desire for a clearer vision of God central to your time with God. Include it in your prayers. Focus your meditations on it.

Let the desire be part of your daily life. Consciously notice the qualities of the Creator revealed in the world and people around you.

Keep a list devoted solely to what you can glean from the sacred texts. Look for direct references to the nature, activity, and qualities of the Almighty. Choose one characteristic at a time and explore it in depth.

In these and other ways, we apply ourselves to seeing God more truly. And we wait for insights and revelations that God alone provides.

We also gain a new view of ourselves.

So much of our self-perception grows out of our experience with other people. Whether family or friends, teachers or colleagues, the people in our lives become a mirror for our sense of self. If we enjoy close associations that are supportive, appreciative, and loving, we may learn to value ourselves as people who can be loved and love in return. If we deal, as the woman in the discussion group did, with abusive close relationships, we may come to see ourselves in a negative light.

As we grow up, new perspective helps us interpret and refine our view of self. We learn to accept or reject the judgments of others. We apply knowledge and a growing store of wisdom. But in all of this, we confine ourselves to finite human understanding. Only in relation to the Divine do we begin to see ourselves as we are seen by God.

The journey toward a true view of ourselves begins when we open ourselves to God's voice. As we consider who and what we are, we prepare for the moments when God says, "Let there be light." We move in the direction of enlightenment when we discover what the Word has to say about us and our relationship with God.

❧ *First, God's Word says, we are loved by God.* God's love, unlike most human love, is unconditional. It doesn't matter what we look like, what sort of personality we have, or how much we've accomplished. According to Scripture, God loves us, each and every one, with a love so personal and infinite that even the hairs on our heads are numbered. We can ask God to help us sense that love as we seek God's presence.

❧ *Second, we are created in the image of God.* Sometimes we look at ourselves with disappointment or dismay. But when we give in to self-loathing, we're sneering at the One who made us. The image of God is within us, no matter how distorted it may be. As we search out God's qualities, we can simultaneously look for the ways in which they exist in our human form, and we can ask God to develop them in us.

🌿 *Third, we are meant to live as those in the company of God.* If we take seriously the One we seek, we will notice those aspects of ourselves and our lives that do not belong in such holy company. Let God bring to your mind those parts of your life that don't "fit" in your Maker's company. These things turn you away from God. The best way to let God redirect you is to confess what's standing in the way and ask forgiveness for it. Here more than anywhere else, we experience transformation. More about this when we consider a transformed heart.

🌿 *Finally, we have been uniquely fashioned with our own set of traits and talents.* Try making a list of what you see as the 10 "most important" features of your personality and temperament—intelligence, friendliness, originality, strength of purpose, optimism, persistence, physical stamina, sense of humor, and so on. Concentrate on the positive. Keep the list beside you during your time with God. Ask God to bring to mind traits that you've missed. Listen for God's view of how those traits might be important in the life you've been given.

A new view of God and ourselves leads us to a new view of others and the world we share.

All that we can say about ourselves in relation to God, we must also acknowledge about others. To look at others with God's eyes is to see beloved children. A friend of mine is presently dealing with an adult daughter who is in acute psychological pain and who has reacted by treating her parents and many of her friends with sometimes irrational disdain and selfishness. The daughter's friends have one by one given up in dismay or retaliated with anger and rejection. Her parents, on the other hand, though often hurt and angry, cannot forget that this is their child. They do not like and sometimes even fear her behavior. But they will not, under any circumstances, stop loving their daughter or longing for change, growth, and eventual happiness for her.

It takes a willing, conscious effort to look for the child of God in other people. It takes a special act of God-sized grace in us to see the beauty and potential within a difficult or unlovely person, particularly someone who is in a position to hurt us or those we love. In such situations, God can strengthen our desire to see others as clearly and lovingly as God sees them, if we bring our desire into our time of prayer and meditation. In the process, we may find that not only are those around us transformed, but we are ourselves.

NEW HEART *Growth of Character*

Out of the human heart—metaphorically the seat of love and morality—emanate our finest hours, our noblest acts of selflessness, our deepest desires, and our darkest wrongdoings.

It is no secret that all is not well with the human heart. Our fine hours are invariably shadowed by our unworthy actions. The Bible writers declare that wrongdoing, referred to as *sin,* is anything we do (or fail to do) that separates us from God, that drives divisions between us and others, that alienates us from creation, or that causes disintegration within ourselves. In the aftermath of wrongdoing, our hearts are broken. Rabbi Nosson Scherman wrote that when we sin without repentance, when we *continue* to sin, we are diminished as human beings. We become indifferent to evil, we tolerate and even develop a taste for it, and we eventually come to dislike good. The rabbis of old called this the "insulation of the heart." Only by rejecting our misdeeds can we open the way for God's love and forgiveness.

With a New Heart

FACE THE WRONG WE'VE DONE

ASK GOD TO ATTUNE US TO GOOD

LOOK FORWARD TO WHOLENESS

The Jewish observance Yom Kippur marks a solemn day of atonement (what some explain as making us "at one" with God). During this occasion, Jews formalize their turning from sin and seeking God's forgiveness. In ancient times in Israel, the priests offered sacrifices signifying that punishment for wrongdoing had been removed from those who sincerely repented; this was the outcome of forgiveness.

The Christian Bible reiterates that God's holiness requires a punishment for sin. Two thousand years ago, John the Baptist saw Jesus coming toward him and declared, "Look, the Lamb of God, who takes away the sin of the world!" Jesus himself proclaimed, "I am the way and the truth and the life. No one comes to the Father except through me." Christians believe that God's love and forgiveness were displayed in Jesus' life, death, and resurrection, so that when he received the punishment for sin on behalf of those who repent, he became the path to divine absolution and connectedness.

If we want our hearts to be transformed, we have to be willing to face the wrong we've done, the good we've avoided, and the wrong that has been done to us. We can reverently approach God without fear, knowing that God loves us and wants to forgive us and make our hearts whole.

As we continue, we can ask God to make us more sensitive to evil and attuned to good. Regrettably, the media give undue emphasis to the evils in the life of our society. Too often, we become desensitized to evil. We come to take it for granted, to believe we can do nothing about it. But just as God gives us new eyes with which to see differently, our Creator can give us a new heart with which to respond differently. When we seek God, we seek a connection to ultimate goodness that we can carry with us into all of life, to face and challenge evil where we find it.

We can turn our attention away from the past and toward a future life that is lived with wholeness of heart and spirit. When we receive God's love and forgiveness, we are set free from the burdens of the past. We can let go of regrets and guilt and shame; we can journey forward with joy. What we are at heart has a profound and growing effect on how we live. A whole heart produces a whole life. A heart truly directed toward God leads us into a life that reflects God's holy character.

NEW HANDS *Freedom to Love & Serve*

The human hand is a miracle of engineering. We have thumbs that allow us to grasp and build, fine motor skills that allow us to accomplish the most intricate of tasks, millions of sensory receivers that let us feel the tiniest texture, and tendons that connect to the larger muscles of arms and shoulders and enable us to do the heavy lifting life often requires. We are surgeons and steelworkers, gardeners and typists, artisans and cooks, and engineers and child-care providers. The miraculous human hand allows us all this and sets us apart from other creatures.

Our hands also provide us with some of our most useful and powerful metaphors. We "reach out" to one another. We "clap hands" in enthusiastic response. We "join hands" in united efforts. We deliver people into "good hands." We "raise our hands" to be counted in support, or we raise our fists in anger. We offer a "helping hand" and the "right hand of fellowship." Bible writers often refer to hands in the context of blessing and of the "laying on of hands."

When we seek God again and again, we not only open our eyes and our hearts to divine influence and transformation but empower our hands to shape our lives in ways that honor our connection with

God. As our perspective is informed by God's point of view, and as our character is mended and matured to better reflect the image of God in us, our life can become the meaningful, important existence we were created to live. And our spirit will be satisfied.

How do we receive new hands?

To begin with, we can apply new understanding and character to the way we are presently living.

I've watched infants grab their own faces and scratch or pinch to the point that they wailed in pain or frustration. Their hands have all the right equipment and connections, but the babies lack the coordination and skills to use them. In God's company, our hands become more skilled; that is, we begin to learn how to apply more of what we have and are to the business of living a life in the presence of the Almighty.

✺ *In your time with God, examine your life as it is.* Are there aspects of how you're living that don't seem to fit anymore? Do you have relationships that seem out of sorts or even wrong? Make these considerations a part of your meditation and prayer.

✺ *If you see changes that need to be made, take the first step.* One small change at a time adds up over time. We can be overwhelmed when we look at everything that needs to be changed at once. When we learn to trust God, we can ask for the wisdom and strength to isolate the changes we're able to make to head ourselves in God's direction. At the same time, we can take note of those changes that have to wait and look forward to making them when the opportunity presents itself.

    Look for aspects of your life that have developed in God's loving care. We can get into such an "overhaul" mind-set that we forget to enjoy the progress we make and the evidence of God's presence. Take time to notice the good that is growing, to be glad and thankful.

We can always ask God to meet us when we experience pain and failure.

The journey toward God often begins with a sense of deep need and longing—when we're seeking relief from pain, whether physical, spiritual, or emotional, because of intellectual or philosophical questions for which we have found no compelling answers. These needs do not automatically go away on the road to God. In fact, new needs invariably crop up. But God is more powerful than our worst crises. When we bring them to our time with God, we seek the strongest, most compassionate, and wisest ally life offers.

    Honestly face the troubling aspects of your life. Put a name to them and consider them in God's presence.

    Consciously, constantly ask for God's help. God is able and willing to make our lives better. Prayer opens the way for divine aid.

    Look for the ways in which you need to participate in the healing and restoring of your life. God has made us conscious and free. We have choices.

When we choose to work *with* God in our lives, we speed the process and grow stronger ourselves.

We can prayerfully look ahead to a fruitful life.

When I look at some of the images the Bible writers used to explore God's activity in our lives—healer, shepherd, builder, gardener—I see pictures of a relationship destined to nurture and shape us into a healthy and meaningful, even fruitful, existence. God intends us to blossom in the life we've been given, and to bear fruit—that is, to have something good and important to show for our lives.

With New Hands

APPLY NEW
UNDERSTANDING
TO LIFE

ASK FOR GOD'S
PRESENCE IN OUR
PAIN AND FAILURE

LOOK AHEAD TO A
FRUITFUL LIFE

I think again of the apple tree, and how my family tended it. We lopped off what was unhealthy so the strong parts of the tree could grow stronger. We removed extra growth to send more of the tree's energy into producing fruit. The tree had its seasons, it weathered its hurricanes, and it had years in which it rested. But we cared for it through it all. When we trimmed or used strong medicine, we did it for the tree's good and for its future. And it became a living symbol of our care.

I imagine God, the divine Gardener, tending us through a lifetime. We certainly experience those times when life seems to be hitting us hard. After seasons of hopes fulfilled and happy occurrences, there may come hazards and sorrows so severe, we wonder whether we can survive them. Yet as we continue to seek God, we have the assurance that nothing in our lives needs to be wasted. God is perfectly good and right and never causes evil. But God can take evil when it befalls us and transform it into a tool for our ultimate growth and well-being. In the ancient story of the Jewish patriarch Joseph, we hear him forgive brothers, who had betrayed him in a terrible way, then asked for his help in a time of dire need. Referring to their treachery, Joseph said to them, "You intended to harm me, but God intended it for good."

We experience our lives as a grand mix of good, bad, and in between. But when we seek God for a lifetime, we can at heart rest in the assurance that God always intends our good. We can come to God alone—simply, honestly, sincerely. But we do not exist alone. We were each of us created a member of the human community, set in a specific historical time and place, and given particular talents, personality, relationships, and inclinations. As our sight becomes clearer, as our hearts mature and heal, our lives have the potential to become the masterpieces—meaningful, beautiful, and important—God desires them to be. And we can experience all that makes up our lives with a simplicity of spirit that bestows a deep and lasting joy.

Meditations

ON TRANSFORMATION

You've come as far as this little guide can take you in drawing close to God. Where will you go from here? God desires your company and your commitment. Will you consider, honestly and purposefully, whether you are presently responding to the urgings of God with clearing vision, a healing heart, and strengthening hands? Remember that every day is both a new beginning and a step further along the path toward God. Let these final meditations and the words of Scripture be an instrument in the long and wonderful process of your transformation.

Day One

One of the most basic tricks in a magician's bag of illusions is people's tendency to see what they expect to see. Sleight of hand depends on it. Sometimes scientists miss important data in an experiment because the results don't conform to what they expect. Sometimes we consider an object lost because we didn't find it where we expected it to be.

Consider today whether your expectations in relation to God may be getting in the way of seeing what God really wants to show you.

BIBLE READINGS

Psalm 17:6-7   Ephesians 1:18-23

Day Two

*I*n *Wishful Thinking,* Frederick Buechner writes, "True repentance spends less time looking at the past and saying, 'I'm sorry,' than to the future and saying, 'Wow!'"

Consider just one area of your life that has necessitated an "I'm sorry" from you. What "Wow!" can you imagine in the future as a result?

BIBLE READINGS

Jeremiah 15:19-21   Acts 3:19-21

Day Three

A number of parrots escaped from a local pet store some years ago. Much to the community's surprise, these exotic birds from the other side of the Equator—destined for cages until their flight—have not only survived, they have thrived and multiplied. Whatever adaptation they needed to set up housekeeping in the huge pine of a New England town they have successfully made. God gave them greater resources than we ever imagined.

Are you facing an unfamiliar place in your life, whether in your relationships, your work, your spiritual life, or your service to others? How might God be preparing you for greater strength and resilience to thrive there?

BIBLE READINGS

Psalm 119:27-32   *Philippians 4:12-13*

Day Four

I sat in a darkening room with some friends one early evening. As dusk fell, Richard reached over and turned the switch on a lamp. Nothing happened. After several tries, he excused himself and went to find a new lightbulb. Soon the old bulb had been removed and the new one screwed into place. Again Richard turned the lamp switch. Again nothing happened. He checked the position of the wall switch that controlled power to the room. It was in the "on" position. He fiddled with the switch. It seemed to be sound. Finally someone asked the obvious question: "Is it plugged in?" A quick trace to the end of the cord behind a chair revealed that the lamp was, in fact, unplugged. Lesson learned: If we want illumination, we need to connect to the source of power.

Reflect on your connection to the Source of life's illumination. If answers seem dim, is it possible you're fiddling with the switch and changing the bulb instead of plugging in?

BIBLE READINGS

2 Samuel 22:29-37   John 12:44-46

Day Five

The photograph on the front page after the latest hurricane showed cauldron waters surging across a roadway and a house knocked sideways off its foundation. In the foreground of the image, three people struggled arm in arm into the wind. I doubt that any of them could have stood, never mind move, if not for the others.

Sometimes we are the arm God offers another to pull him or her through the storm. Reflect on the people in your life today. Is God extending a helping hand to you through one of them? Might you be the one who can offer God's aid?

BIBLE READINGS

Leviticus 18:9-18   *Galatians 5:13-14*

Day Six

We have new twins in the family, identical little girls. In all their parts they match, with nothing to distinguish them. Except this: They have their own fingerprints. God has made their hands distinct in this way. And each one of them has her own unique part to play in this life.

Take time today to consider your unique place in the universe. Ask God to help you see all you can be.

BIBLE READINGS

Proverbs 16:3-4   Philippians 2:12-16

Day Seven

You'd never guess to look at it that an egg is home to a living creature. When a chick hatches—a naked, scrawny nestling—you'd never guess to look at it that it could one day soar on its own wings to the top of a mountain. We assume too much from the bare appearances of things. God knows what's coming.

Remember today to be thankful for all you will yet become. Anticipate it with joy. Serve the Lord with gladness.

BIBLE READINGS

Psalm 95:1-7   Romans 31-39

One thing I ask of the Lord,
   this is what I seek:
that I may dwell
   in the house of the Lord
   all the days of my life,
to gaze upon the beauty of the Lord
   and to seek him in his temple.
For in the day of trouble
   he will keep me safe
   in his dwelling;
he will hide me in the shelter
   of his tabernacle
   and set me high upon a rock.

Psalm 27:4-5